The
Unicorn Project

Insider Secrets of Senior Living
Plus the Ultimate Step-by-Step Guide
to Assisted Living

DAVID SLOMOVIC

© 2017 by David Slomovic. All rights reserved.

ISBN: 0692879390
ISBN-13: 978-0-692-87939-9

Books may be purchased at AMAZON.COM or at
www.unicornseniorliving.com

No part of this book may be reproduced in any written, electronic, recording, or photocopying form without written permission of the author, David Slomovic.

DEDICATIONS

I wish to make multiple dedications of this book, as it is fitting and necessary for me to thank and recognize those who have made it possible. Giving credit where credit is due does not occur often enough, so I am going to do it here. As in my life and career, I am going to do what I want and think is right and let the chips fall where they may.

First, I wish to thank the staff and residents who trusted me with their future for nearly eighteen years. Just as you do not know what life is about until you have children, you do not know what working is about until you have employees and their lives depend on you. It was an honor and a privilege to serve you.

Second, this book was not my idea. Joan Waltman, the brilliant mentor I was lucky enough to find during my days as a senior-living-community owner and operator, has been a guide, illuminator, visionary, and friend who assisted me in overcoming my many limitations, and I will be forever grateful.

Third, my beautiful wife, Tammy, and my three delicious children, Julia, Billy, and Zachary, all provided me with a measure of patience and understanding as I came to the office to write on weekends and late at night. Never once did they complain about my driving need to birth this book. I love and treasure each one of you and thank you.

Fourth, my love to the only grandparent I have ever known, Gizella Berkovitz. Her love, affection, and warmth have always given me strength and confidence.

The final dedication is to my late father and mother, Jack and Miriam Slomovic. No one on earth was blessed with better parents, and their love and belief in me are the only reasons I am who I am today. My love and respect for them know no boundaries, and they are with me always.

"There are those who look at things the way they are and ask *why?* I dream of things that never were, and ask *why not?*"

Robert Francis Kennedy

CONTENTS

INTRODUCTION

I have always considered myself the luckiest guy in the world, which is strange because I do not believe in luck. I have also always taken the road less traveled. So when my unusual journey took me from being a passionate trial attorney in criminal law to being a protector of seniors in a senior-living community, there was no precedent I could find. Simply put, I have always been the underdog, and I have always sought to protect and defend the underdog. There was no playbook to study. No blueprint to follow. I used same process of analysis that had served me well my entire life. This meant figuring it all out on the fly based on silent observation, conclusions based on logic, and the timeless values my parents had taught me. With that combination, I was unstoppable.

Until I was stopped cold. I was stopped by everyone and everything that saw me as an outsider, as a pretender, and as a threat. To me, from the beginning senior living was suffering from a core disconnect. It was not about the seniors at all, which is why senior living has failed to get the proper traction in our society, or the world, for that matter. Senior living is the only industry in which almost no one asks customers what they want or if they are happy with the product. There is currently no national standard for senior-living communities. I will explain why this is so later, but this is essentially why senior living has been consistently rejected by approximately 90 percent of eligible seniors and their families for what will be next year my twentieth year in this complex and convoluted space.

At a recent senior-living conference that I attended, the keynote speaker lamented that we have only a 10 percent penetration rate in the market, meaning only one out of ten eligible seniors lives in senior living. She added that if only 1 percent more of seniors moved into a community, every single bed in America would be filled. I have no idea if these numbers are true, but everyone at my table, all senior-living professionals, debated the reasons for this as if we were discussing life on Mars. One lady asked me if I had a guess as to why so few people want to live in senior living. I said that I knew exactly why nine out of ten people do not live with us. They laughed, like they could not wait for this false oracle to give a silly answer. "So tell us," one lady said with a smile, "tell us why we have only a ten percent penetration into the market."

"I can do it with one simple question," I stated.

"Really," she said with a snicker, "I'm dying to hear this."

"It is very simple," I said. "How many of you ladies plan to live in the communities you operate?" The smiles disappeared.

"Well," she began, "I purchased a home in Florida last year to be near my—"

I cut her off and pointed to the next lady. "How about you?" I went one by one at the table. Each had a different excuse or deflection. "You see? None of you do. And you know why? Because senior living is just not good enough for you. That's why. Because we make it just good enough for others, but not good enough for us. That is the key flaw, and why we are stuck at ten percent. On average, as an industry, we don't make the living conditions worthy of living in the places we run, own, or work at." One by one, they left the table until I was alone.

The truth is that these are good people, and senior living is mostly staffed by deeply caring people who chose this space because they care and love seniors. And therein lies the problem. They think they are doing a great job because the industry numbers are robust, the money flows, they love to give each other awards and celebrate transactions, growth, and mergers, and yet something crucial is missing. Senior living has no soul. There, I said it. Someone had to.

After my nearly eighteen years running a community, and nineteen years overall in this space, the time has come to share the many wonderful and horrible moments experienced and witnessed. As an outsider, I came in knowing less than nothing, and I left nearly two decades later feeling as if I were David in Wonderland having gone through the rabbit hole and come out the other side loaded with secrets and experiences no one would believe.

In criminal law, I learned early on that eyewitness testimony is the least reliable form of accurate evidence. So I humbly state that this book is a reflection of my memory as to how things happened. I do not guarantee perfect accuracy; in fact, it is more likely that the march of time and perhaps a few cocktails have dimmed the precision of what exactly happened. Recognizing this fallibility is important—in most of the cases here, the point is not the exact wording or the exact time or location, but rather the lesson and the wisdom gleaned from the experience.

So buckle up, as there are twists and turns awaiting you. Yes, it is going to be a bumpy ride, but upon finishing this book, you will have more knowledge than 90 percent of the executive directors (EDs) you are going to meet in this industry. You will know exactly what to look for in a community, what clues tell you if the community you are in or are considering is the right one for you. You will know how to negotiate the best rates and services, and you will learn the warning signs of troubled communities and how to steer clear of them. You will learn how to stand up for yourself or your loved one if there are problems, and you will learn the dirty little secrets that only insiders know, so you can intelligently and successfully navigate these murky waters. You will likely find one of the many wonderful communities staffed by caring angels who will enhance your life and extend the quality of it. Read this book and emerge as the hero of your life, or be the hero of the life of someone you love and adore.

The big question is, has the billion-dollar senior-living industry (SLI) done it "right," and is it gaining approval by fulfilling its promises to do the right things and make the proverbial golden years actually golden?

Perhaps I am wrong and am a crazy rogue critic who exited the industry by sheer dumb luck and have no idea what I am talking about when I say that the senior-living machine is failing and doing much of it the wrong way by focusing almost exclusively on all the wrong things.

Perhaps, but recently my wife and I were channel surfing, and *Celebrity Family Feud* popped up, so we watched for a few minutes. A question was posed something like this: "We got the top four answers to this question. We asked one hundred people, 'Where do you expect to be on your one hundredth birthday?'" The contestants buzzed in.

"Assisted living!" I yelled.

"Of course, you would say that," my wife muttered with a smile.

"Dead," said the player with a big smile. Bing! Number-one answer. The family decided to play.

The next family member was up. "Senior living!" I yelled.

"Home," the contestant said. Bing! Number two.

"Independent living!" I shouted so loud my three dogs glared at me.

"Hospital," the next contestant said. Bing! Number three.

One answer left. Host Steve Harvey went to the next contestant and asked the question again. The family kept guessing wrong. "Retirement home!" I yelled in total frustration. No one guessed the final one, and Harvey was forced to reveal the final answer. Bing!

"Disney World."

It is unconscionable that in a question directed specifically to the housing of seniors that senior living was *not mentioned by one person*. That, my friends, is a reflection of the total failure of an entire industry.

This book is an invitation to join me in my quest to pull back the Gray Curtain and seek the truth and learn the secret skills and hidden clues needed to effectively care for our most fragile and complex citizens. Together we can educate people (and perhaps shift and disrupt the industry's focus) so that our elders are once again cherished and respected and given the honor, respect, and dignity they so very much deserve. It must finally happen.

So let us begin where it all began.

Chapter 1
ASSUMPTIONS

In early 1998 I sat down after an emotional and detailed ninety-minute closing argument defending a young man in a murder trial at the Santa Monica Courthouse. I had no idea that, thirty days later, I would walk away from a promising law career to help my family run a struggling senior-living business. I am probably the only person in the world who went from trial attorney in criminal law to senior-care advocate overnight. What I knew about senior living, like most people, could not fill a thimble. But, somehow, over the next eighteen years, I fell in love with the senior-living world and with caring for and empowering seniors to live happier, safer, and more fulfilling lives.

Why did I do it? The truth is that my beloved mother and father planted the seeds of respecting my elders early and by example. I learned from my family that time is precious. It is the omnipresent disruptor and the most valuable of all commodities. It is the thing we cherish the most and manage the worst. And all the while, the clock never stops ticking.

My father was a builder of both businesses and people. In the early 1970s, he built Golden Gate Lodge, a large adult-living facility for seniors on Venice Boulevard in Los Angeles. I was probably seven or eight years old when he built Golden Gate, and I clearly remember standing on plywood three floors off the ground in a wood-framed building, across the street from the giant Helms Bakery. I walked up the steps and smelled the sweet aroma of sawdust. I stood on wood planks on the top floor without a roof, and I felt like the king of the world.

My father was the owner and builder, and I watched it slowly get built, week by week. I thought he was the greatest man alive, building places where people lived their lives. I loved going with my dad to the job site.

When construction was completed and the interior finished, I got to see new employees hired and people start to move in. It was exciting. He had created a little world for his new residents, a place for them to enjoy their lives.

On Sundays I often would tag along with my dad. He would typically walk in from the garage parking lot and head straight to the main office to see Eli, my uncle. Eli, one of my mother's brothers, was the administrator. He had pleasant people skills, was extraordinarily organized, and was completely trustworthy. I would walk around the building by myself while they were talking.

Straight ahead from the garage exit was a little walkway leading to the back entrance of the building and the back of the kitchen. Past that, resident rooms could be found to the left and right. If I veered left, right after going past a storage closet and office, I would come to the first resident room. In it sat a man, always in the same chair, always with his back to the door, always staring out the window. Whenever I came there, I would walk up to his open door and watch him stare outside, wondering what in the world he was looking at. No matter when I went, he was always there, looking out his window.

One day he said, "You can come in if you want, you know."

He never turned to look at me, so I wasn't sure whom he was talking to. I looked around, but I was the only one there, so I figured he was talking to me.

"It's okay; you can come in if you like," he repeated.

I had always wondered what he was looking at. I walked up next to him in his chair by the window and looked to see if maybe there was a cat, dog, bird, or something so very interesting, but I didn't see anything.

I asked, "What are you always looking at all the time?"

He said, "What do you mean?"

I said, "It's just a wall and a gate and the garage. Why do you stare at it all the time? Nothing is happening. What is so interesting?"

He paused, smiled slightly, and said, "I am blind. I'm not looking at anything at all. I cannot see. I just like the feeling of the warm sun on my face, and I can hear the comings and goings."

I had never met a blind person before and wasn't sure how I was supposed to act. I asked him if being blind hurt, and he laughed and gently said, "No."

From that day on, whenever I visited with my dad, I would go to see him first. We would talk about things I saw and did. I would describe them to him in detail. He liked that. He cared about not just *what* I saw but *how* I saw the world. I liked him and how he treated me like a real person, not just like a little kid. I looked forward to seeing him. Sometimes I would be sneaky and creep in slowly to try and surprise him, and he would suddenly say, "Good morning, David."

Sometimes he would ask me to read to him. He was interested in the world through my eyes and taught me how to really listen to other people and to the world. I was grateful to have such a wise and nice old friend. He was Yoda before there was a Yoda. I cherished our special friendship and learned many things from him.

One day I walked in, but something was off. The room was different. The bed was made like new. The air smelled of disinfectant, the chair was at the table, and the shade was closed. He was not there.

I asked the nurse where he was. She was a lovely large older black lady that I had known a long time.

She replied, "He's gone, baby."

"Gone where? When's he coming back?"

"Oh, he's not coming back, baby."

"Why not?" I asked. "Where did he go? I need to know," I pleaded.

She walked over, patted me on the head, and said with a kind smile, "He's not coming back because he died and went to heaven, and he's with God now."

I had no idea what that meant, but I remember how it felt. It felt cold and scary and sad, and I wanted to go home immediately. He was my only grown-up friend, and I was pretty sure that I was his only kid friend. And we never even got to say good-bye.

Chapter 2
THE MISSION

My core mission is to assist you in navigating the confusing senior-living waters so that you make informed decisions and locate the right community for yourself or your loved one. I will show you how to maximize your dollars, make the transition as painless and free of landmines as possible, and increase the probability of success. My mission is to help you and your family understand and benefit from what I know, and use it to create the best possible reality for those you love.

How will this daunting task be accomplished? By lifting the veil of secrecy and going behind the Gray Curtain—sharing inside information and hidden secrets about how senior living works and how to make it work for you. Senior living truly is a far better life for most elderly people. This opinion is based on personal observations; I no longer have a horse in this race and am not motivated to fill my community. But I have seen so many seniors arrive as withered souls and, months later, seen them laughing with new friends. This change is not only a testimony to the greatness of the people who work in this difficult space, but it's also incredibly satisfying for me. I am a proud and unrepentant senior-living evangelist because seeing older people get happy is addictive and perhaps the most joyous thing I have ever known.

This book will hopefully help more families move into senior living to enjoy their lives. It offers a better social life, more happiness, greater safety, a potential elongation of the "quality" years, and increased peace of mind for all members of the family. In the end, you will shine if you follow the instructions and be the savior for someone who does not even realize he or she needs saving.

But I must admit that I have an ulterior motive. If I'm lucky, one day I will want to live in a senior-living community. It will be my world, and I want it to be better. Not just better, but truly amazing. So amazing that people cannot wait to get old. That is what I want. That would be the opposite of how everything is today. It all begins with a simple yet critical question:

What if we could recalibrate our relationship with aging?

What if we could make old age the greatest time in our life? What if senior living were the finish line where you were amply rewarded for enduring the endless hardships of life, for a lifetime of devotion to the family, for toiling at a job for fifty years, for making good health, food, and life decisions, and for simply surviving the gauntlet of life itself? What if it were the prize for winning the race?

What if we could, for the first time ever, make the golden years truly golden?

Wouldn't that logically make perfect sense? The goal of nearly all living creatures is to reproduce and survive as long as possible. In the days of early humanity, managing to hit your twenties was a miracle. In Greek and Roman times, life expectancy for most was between twenty and thirty-five. In the Middle Ages, people who made it to their forties were considered wise and blessed (they had survived the bubonic plague). Life expectancy in 1850 was forty, and by 1900, it had jumped to forty-seven. But in 2007, with the improvements in living conditions, medicine, and nutrition, life expectancy reached seventy-eight years. And (spoiler alert!) life expectancy is still going to increase, bringing with it maximum life expectancy, which has been surpassed again and again. The number of centenarians (people over one hundred) is increasing at approximately 5.5 percent per year, resulting in a doubling of the centenarian population every thirteen years, pushing it from 450,000 in 2009 to a projected 4.1 million in 2050. **Think about that number for a moment and let it sink in.** Note: I played the citation game in law for many years, so you are just going to have to trust me with all these figures, but feel free to do your own research.

Recent books state that babies born today could live to be 150 years old. We have entered the golden age of aging, and yet no one seems to know it, let alone want to celebrate. All of this sounds like science fiction, but it is more about science enabling us to live longer. But will we simply live longer, or will we live both longer *and* better?

My mission, which I feel I have no choice but to accept, is to make senior living and getting older the very best time of your entire life. Quite ambitious, I admit, but, logically, why shouldn't it be? A lifetime of pressure is finally off. The mountain of work is behind you. The kids, if you have them, are launched, and hopefully you are in pure grandparent mode. You have time, presumably planned well, and you have money, and hopefully you even have the energy to enjoy both.

Death is no longer the thief taking such a high percentage of people so early. The opposite is true today. People are actually outliving their bodies now. The massive increase of Alzheimer's and Parkinson's cases reflect new challenges that show the other side of the shift in life expectancy.

In addition, medical research is pushing the boundaries even further, not to mention the benefits of technology to counteract many of the diminishing abilities seniors face. There is tremendous attention on baby boomers and the predicted "Silver Tsunami" as they leave the workforce. So everyone is thrilled, right?

Wrong. People are absolutely terrified. People are terrified to get older now, and the older people are scared of their future. The main reason for this is constant negative imagery. Television, movies, books, advertising, and magazines have told you a million times that aging is bad and to be avoided at all costs. These messages are designed so that you buy products to keep you looking young even if you are not young at all. This seismic shift in our social psychology pushes you to buy special makeup, moisturizers, skin care and antiwrinkle creams, dietary supplements, and vitamins, and has also given rise to innumerable antiaging institutes, clinics, and longevity and age-management centers. Add to that the enormous business of plastic surgery, Botox, skin tightening, implants, and weight loss. Notice a trend here? Making you feel bad about yourself is big business. Your insecurities have produced a billion-dollar industry.

We have been tricked into rejecting the most natural thing in the world: aging. Aging is not a disease or an illness, but it has been perfectly framed like one. And, worse yet, the marketing message drummed into your head a hundred times every day is that getting older is actually your fault. We have almost portrayed aging as a crime. The motivation is pure financial greed. And everyone is buying it, literally.

In 2008, the global amount spent on antiaging products and services was a stunning $162 billion. A mere five years later, this global industry market was estimated to be a mind-boggling **$261.9 billion—in a single year.**

All this despite the fact that everyone knows that one cannot reverse aging. Yet people run to buy the latest product that claims to contain bottled youth. To give you some perspective on these numbers, in 2014 the United States spent $35 billion on foreign economic aid for the entire world. We are spending like crackheads for products and solutions we know don't work. But we cannot stop. We have become addicted.

So why are we doing it? Fear. Pure, brilliantly marketed fear playing on our insecurities, especially those of women. A fear developed and nurtured by people selling antiaging serums. What was once called "snake oil" is now called a "breakthrough in antiaging technology."

And, as always, the United States leads the way. In my humble opinion, this country has been most unkind to seniors, and horrible to women in particular. I would have written "to aging women," but that would be an "insult." Later you will read my breakdown of how we have been duped into marginalizing all that is older without even realizing it. Our elders and symbols of older people these days are no longer revered or admired like George Washington and Ben Franklin. They are spoofed and denigrated like Archie Bunker and Abe Simpson.

So how are we going to accomplish this enormous mission? It shall be no easy task. I wish to recalibrate the core flaw in the senior-living formula. Time itself is the key. We need to treasure it as we have all been given a certain amount of time to enjoy life. Are we really going to spend our later years yearning for what we had in our youth, or will we treasure our time and maximize it?

I envision a completely different world inhabited by the elderly—a world of **opportunity, safety, inclusion, and wonder**. A world in which they are surrounded by beauty, comforts, and the best of all things as they adapt to their changing needs. I see a world in which individuals envision their favorite things and then receive them by truckloads. Love bridge? Live in a community that obsesses on bridge and has progressively larger cards so you can continue to play as your eyesight declines. Love yoga? Move to a community that has yoga coming out of every pore. Into sports? Singing? Art?

Bocce ball? Whatever your passion, you should live in a place that has it in spades. Retiring should be like graduating and going to Disneyland for prom, but you get to stay and live there **forever**.

It should be the ultimate E ticket ride, but that is the exact opposite of everything you and everyone else think and understand about senior living. And senior living is guilty as charged. First of all, despite different names, colors, and flags, nearly every community is the same: same amenities, apartment sizes, food programs, activities, entertainment, and mentalities. They offer "signature" programs or unique names for spaces, services, or staff positions, but it is mostly the same song. Each has a different logo, marketing story, tagline, glossy brochure, and pricing, but they are merely upscale copies of a McDonald's. I'll have a McSenior sandwich, hold the onions and the sadness.

But at least they cater to you and your needs, right? **Uh, wrong again.** Most demand you fit *their* model, not the other way around. They tell you when to eat, shop, and bathe, and tell you what you will eat, who will entertain you, and when the van can pick you up. What this means is that senior living is the one remaining area in which the customer does not control his or her life or choices. And therein lies the problem, and the core reason why senior living has roughly only a 10 percent penetration rate, meaning only one in ten seniors live in senior living. I wholeheartedly believe that for most people, senior living is 80 percent better than aging in place, alone in an empty house, with nothing to do and little to look forward to.

So imagine a world in which you finally hit a certain age and decide you want to be dedicated to your oil painting, which you have put off for fifty years. Or you love dogs and move into a community full of pets, with a dog park and acres of outside space for you and your dog to enjoy. Senior living should be a clear upgrade—the end of dragging groceries up and down, the end of cleaning, washing dishes, and calling unknown repairmen. Instead, it is the time for you to be who you always wanted to be and to do what you always wanted to do. It is not too late.

But the senior-living industry chooses to not go or grow in this direction. Perhaps they cannot see the bottom-line impact, or they lack the ability to imagine it. Perhaps mechanically or operationally, it is erroneously believed not to be cost effective or is too narrow somehow or too financially risky. Perhaps they simply do not want to give up control. And that is where we come in, because part of this mission is to convince the senior-living industry that evolving into a more customer-centric model will be not only morally right but a financial bonanza. It does not have to be one or the other. It can and should be both. I proved that.

So why has this not happened? Two key reasons. The first is that the Internet funnels controlling the flow and path of potential customers are not always focused on the best interest of the family or the resident looking for an ideal solution and the right fit. **Referral agencies** are enormously powerful but unrecognized players in the senior-living machine. These referral companies are mostly all the same in what they do, and there is little effort in matching the resident with the right community. This huge undiagnosed problem with senior and assisted living results in a massive amount of resident and family dissatisfaction.

Google searches are the other big engine here. They put you in the position of being bombarded with prepackaged information that is either completely one-sided or completely reactionary. Neither works well to produce the desired result of finding the right match between person and place.

The second reason this has not happened is because everyone, including you, feels, deep down, that senior living is the place you go to die. Sorry for the blunt talk, but everyone views it as the end of the road. Yes, seniors die and are closer to the end than the beginning, but that is the core misperception. Senior living is the only place I have seen people come back to life and find their purpose and their joy. Could it be better? Of course. The bottom line is that for most, moving to senior living is **an upgrade** in fun, safety, health, and peace of mind. It is simply a better life and a solution for most. Imperfect, yes, but superior.

Today we are blessed with the most advanced medicine and technology the world has ever known. Are we really going to focus on hating the laugh lines we spent a lifetime acquiring? Worse yet, seniors and their families have been sold the biggest lie of all: **the best thing an adult child of a senior can do is to have a parent age in place.**

This means that the senior should stay in the same house the entire family lived in fifty years ago and pretend that nothing has changed as a sign of strength and independence. This load was brought to you by people who have a vested interest in you staying home alone when you are old. These same people then try to sell you home health-care services, senior-care products, or special equipment designed to keep you "independent."

The typical marketing hook is deeply emotional, manipulative, and effective: This is your home, where your memories are and where you are safe. Move away, and the memories and your entire existence disappear. That is a powerful message to someone who has endured loss. It does not matter that your home, where four or more people may once have lived, now has only one inhabitant, with the other person being a paid caregiver. It is the "die with your boots on" strategy. At its core, the message is that you must live in the past because you have zero future.

This, to me, is both false and evil because the truth is that most seniors end up living alone in quiet isolation, unhappy, often undiagnosed with depression, and extremely vulnerable with no safety net. I have heard every marketing story about why aging in place is wonderful, but it is much like Bigfoot: we have all heard the tale, but no one has ever actually seen one.

The illusion that living alone is safer is perfectly embodied in a product we have all seen a thousand times. They sell a pendant aimed at seniors living alone, with the tagline "I live alone, but I'm never alone. I have product X." These brilliant marketers, who also coined "Help! I've fallen, and I can't get up!" have probably made gazillions of dollars pushing the idea that you are not alone, when in fact you are 100 percent alone.

Yes, there is someone somewhere who I assume will respond to the call, and hopefully the product works. I'm sure in some cases it has saved lives. My aunt had this product, as her children lived out of state and out of the country. She mostly refused to wear it. I saw it on the table numerous times and would strongly suggest she wear it. She told me her children had insisted on it, and she did it to make them happy but did not like it. She also told me that once she fell and could not reach it, and once she pushed the button in pain, and it did not work. I do not know these things for a fact, but I had no reason to doubt her. Bottom line is that this product, like so many others related to seniors, is an illusion of safety and independence, whereas if you live in a community, people check on you and notice if you do not show up to a meal.

Isolation and loss of the social element are the most important factors affecting happiness in seniors. Being alone is the worst thing for most people, and living alone in the shell of your former life seems more like a punishment or a prison than a reward to me. In fact, I have repeatedly seen people aging in place, who had nothing to look forward to and little interaction with others, blossom once they were in a senior community and around other people. Not always, but the vast majority of the time, they slowly came back to life by having regular meals, social interaction, help with their medications, exercise, and entertainment. We are not talking about *Cocoon* here, where the elderly go back to being and feeling young, but we are talking about a fun, safe, and more fulfilling life that helps these wonderful people, who have done so much for so many, have more satisfying and fulfilling lives.

We need to make senior living brilliant. In the past, activity programs I designed brought joy, happiness, and lifelong learning to our clients. These programs included Senior Boot Camp, the Senior Prom, Young at Art, and Dream Makers, to name a few.

I see senior living of the future having laughter coaching, grief counseling, fulfillment coaching, massage therapy, aromatherapy, beauty bars, oxygen bars and that is just the tip of my iceberg.

And that is just the beginning of the journey we will take together. I will be **your dedicated and personal Sherpa**—your guide as you seek to climb these Himalayas. I will be with you every step of the way and open up this world and explain everything to bring you safety to the mountaintop. Once there, it will be up to you.

Aging is mostly a blessing when you consider the alternative. For those who do not share this view, we can make it an enjoyable time of discovery and enlightenment. We can end the isolation and fear. Join me in preventing a life of quiet desperation by stepping up and providing our elders a better life than *Wheel of Fortune* and cold TV dinners. By helping them, you will show them, yourself, and your children that helping a loved one by sacrificing time, effort, and personal comfort for them is **what being a real hero is all about**.

So don't believe the hype. **Getting old is not a crime.** Living alone is a punishment for most, not a reward. These pain points were simply designed to separate you from your cash. They are not true. But one thing that is true is when I was a child there was a wonderful old man who lived down the block, whom everyone called "the Captain." He was a huge, hulking, barrel-chested man with striking white hair under a captain's hat. He was generally found smiling and carrying around a tiny white poodle. On his garage door, he had a handwritten sign that I have never forgotten: **"Don't grow up. It's a trap."**

Let us escape the trap together. The way to do that is to make getting old as great, if not better, as being young. Then, perhaps, we can abandon this illogical and unhealthy obsession about going backward and embrace going forward. My father used to tell me, "You cannot live in the past." He was right.

Do not regret growing older. It is a privilege denied to many. Remember that with age comes wisdom, and I prefer wisdom and thus love being older. Yes, I said the words you have never heard before. I love getting older. I also believe strongly in what George Eliot wrote, which is that it is never too late to be who you might have been.

Hence, the Unicorn Project. The Unicorn Project is my dream of a senior utopia in which older people live together in a beautiful, happy, safe, fulfilling, and harmonious space designed to meet their unique needs and interests. Where the right people are matched and living in the right communities, and we finally discard this medieval "one size fits all" model. Where new technology and modern care meet to maximize declining physical abilities. Where the critical human-touch element and social interactions calm and soothe the soul.

Unicorns are fabled creatures that symbolize magical beauty, power, and purity. I titled this the Unicorn Project because these kinds of senior-living communities and systems simply do not exist. Nor do unicorns. Seniors deserve it, and it is now up to us. **It is time.**

Chapter 3
THE BASEMENT

Leaving law in 1998 was like careening off the freeway at a hundred miles an hour, and downshifting into senior living was like driving on a crowded sidewalk.

A week after quitting my law practice, I drove to our business headquarters on Robertson Boulevard in Los Angeles, settled into my huge, new desk in my huge, new office, got a yellow pad of paper, asked my father what I should do, and asked when he was ready to show me the ropes.

He told me no one had trained him, that he was not going to train me, and that I should get in the car and drive to Fullerton, the city in Orange County where our struggling senior-living community was located.

I had been there once, perhaps ten years before, at the grand opening. Not only did I not remember it, but I couldn't recall where Fullerton even was. I had to use a Thomas Guide to find it, for those who know what that is. I asked what I was going to do there when I arrived. He told me to call him.

So I got in the car and drove to the Sunny Crest Chalet Retirement Residence, which years later I would rename Sunnycrest Senior Living.

In 1998, there was no such thing as "senior living." A facility such as this was called a retirement home, or an old folks' home. In actuality, all of these places were considered a senior's "final stop." The end of the road.

They were depressing places, where the unfortunate few went when they had no one to take care of them or were too difficult for family to deal with. While many in the building were, in fact, retirees, the idea was that this type of establishment was a cheaper alternative to a nursing home.

Over my nearly eighteen years in this space, I would see the nomenclature and purpose of these facilities change from retirement home to independent living to assisted living to the current thinking, senior living. These changes have overlapped and muddied the waters for an audience that finds themselves already confused and stressed about having to make a decision, usually under tremendous pressure. **These ever-changing names are a reflection of the lack of vision, purpose, and core identity of elder care.**

I drove the hour to Sunnycrest, a Residential Care Facility for the Elderly (RCFE), and walked in.

Sunnycrest was nicer than I remembered, although the

> **TIP:** In California, Title 22 of the Health and Safety Code defines the rules and regulations of senior-living communities, and RCFE is a technical term used by professionals and state licensing to categorize this particular level of care. If you are having the discussion with a representative of a community, and you properly use the term RCFE, they will know you are educated and not a simpleton.

mauve-antique look of the place seemed dreary. When I walked in, everyone stopped breathing. I was in one of my trial suits with my favorite suspenders and tie.

"One of the owners is here," I heard someone whisper as they bounced into each other and shuffled around, trying to look busy.

I quickly realized that we were absentee owners, which was a big reason we were failing. My father's weekly visits had not been enough to inspire the staff to greatness, probably because they knew when he was coming, so they put on a show when he was in the building.

I proceeded to the office of the Sunnycrest administrator, Georgette (not her real name). The names have been changed to protect the guilty.

> **TIP:** Each community (I dislike the word "facility" and refuse to use it) must have a licensed administrator, officially designated as an executive director, who is someone with a certain amount of experience and has passed a test given by state licensing. This person is the head of the operation and the only one you really want to deal with. Bad places will insist you deal with the marketing person. No, thank you. They are trained salespeople who have learned how to use the love of your family against you. Avoid them and insist on speaking to the administrator or executive director. When you need something later, the marketing person will be busy, useless or, more likely, no longer there. Connecting with the executive director is key.

Georgette was a very experienced administrator, as exemplified by her many years of service. She knew the field, but she did not know me. No one went in to warn her before I walked into her office, and by the size of her, I don't think she left that office to walk around very often.

The moment I approached, she closed the open window on her computer screen. I introduced myself.

She seemed confused and looked very nervous.

I explained that I had left my law practice and was going to be assisting my father and the company in any way I could.

After thanking her, I went to my father's office (he kept a small office at every property so he would have a presence and a place to sit and work) and called him. I asked him what I was doing there.

He told me to go to the basement and call him from there.

"Why?" I asked.

"Just do it," he said. So I did.

Walking around was strange, knowing that I was a part owner but having no idea where anything was, let alone that we even had a basement.

I had never done anything to contribute to the family business, so I very much welcomed this opportunity to help. My assumption was I was going to assist the marketing staff to bring in new residents and help grow the business.

Upon finding the basement, I located the phone (this was before cell phones) and called headquarters. My father asked, "What do you see?"

I looked around. I was alone in a storage space. "Nothing. There is nothing and no one here."

"What do you see?" he asked in an agitated voice.

"Nothing. There is nothing going on here, Dad."

"What do you see, David?" he repeated even more impatiently.

"I don't know," I said. "Mops? Cans of food? Adult diapers? Toilet paper?"

"I want you to count all the toilet paper."

Neither of us spoke for a while.

"You know, Dad, it's funny. It sounded like you said you wanted me to count the toilet paper."

He said, "That is exactly what you are going to do."

I was stunned. I took a deep breath and said, "Dad, I imagine there are other people here capable of counting toilet paper. May I respectfully remind you that I am a felony trial attorney?"

This was a very touchy moment in our relationship in which my status as a professional and his perception of me as an overgrown child collided at supersonic speed.

"That does not matter," he began. "You don't know anything about this business or any business. So you need to start here and learn each and every job in the building to understand how things work, because one day I will not be here, and you will have to run it yourself, and I will not be there to help. If you do not start at the bottom and learn how each and every job works to make the business work, you will not earn the respect of the staff, and not know how to run it. So start counting the toilet paper, and then count the mops, all the cans of food, and everything in that storage area. Then you will learn to do the inventory; then you will learn ordering. Next you will learn accounting; you will learn to do the books and how to pay the bills. You will learn scheduling, marketing, and so on. So start counting the toilet paper!"

Click. He hung up. I was in shock. Not only had he never hung up on me, but this was an entirely different "Dad." In fact, this was not "Dad." This was Jack. This was the no-excuses, no-hand-holding, take-no-prisoners version of my father I had heard about but never witnessed.

I do not know how long I held that phone in my hand, but it was a while.

Standing in the basement, I realized this was never going to work, that quitting law was a horrible mistake, and that I needed to call my old boss up and accept his offer to come back should this "experiment" not work for me.

I went back upstairs and walked around the building through the alley to the administrator's office. Her desk faced the door, and her back was to the window. As I passed the window to go speak with her, I could see she was not working on her computer but was playing a game of solitaire.

I walked into her office, told her I was leaving, said good-bye, and walked out.

They had no idea what was happening. I was history.

I got in my car, took off my suit jacket, loosened my tie, and prepared to go back to my previous life. I could not believe my father. My mind was racing. I got about three blocks away before I calmed down.

While I was stopped, waiting for the light to turn, his full plan started to crystalize in my mind, and I began to understand what he was actually trying to do.

He was trying to help me the only way he knew how, by throwing me into the fire and forcing me to start at the bottom. He was teaching me the fastest way he knew how. It was a lesson that would serve me very well, even after he was gone.

At that moment, the choice in front of me became clear. I may have pounded my steering wheel a few times, and perhaps said some words I should not have, but I turned that car around. I drove back with my tail between my legs.

When I got back to Sunnycrest, I adjusted my suit, calmly walked in, went down to the basement, took off my jacket, loosened my tie, and, without a word, proceeded to count the toilet paper.

No one knew what to make of my working there. For the first few weeks, the staff looked stunned and avoided me. I did as I was told. Dad told me to keep my mouth shut and my eyes and ears open.

I learned how to do the inventory, ordering, accounting, and so forth. I learned we were not comparing prices, just buying whatever the reps told us we should buy. I quickly discovered the food was horrible as well.

Truth was, everyone there was on autopilot. They did things a certain way because that was how it had always been done. Nearly all of our employees had come from a corporate RCFE background and went about their work in a robotic way. That, by the way, is a symptom of the disease and one of the biggest issues preventing senior living from positively moving forward.

Within six months I had studied and learned the entire operation. I got involved with food planning, preparation, and plate delivery, working with the staff in the kitchen and dining room, and in the dietary department selecting recipes and menus. I also worked with the activities department organizing and creating social events. I learned the names and jobs of each employee, got to know all the residents' names, and lent a hand pushing wheelchairs when needed. I participated in and observed dozens of on-site tours. I took the administrator's exam to ensure I understood the rules and regulations and learned about state licensing.

After those six months, I had a pretty good sense as to why the business was failing: except for a couple of the caregivers, no one gave a damn. It was pathetic and demoralizing. The realization crushed my soul.

TIP: When you go in to visit, check to see if any of the staff are sitting and talking with the residents. If they are, that's a very good sign; it means there are enough staff members present and that they can also take a personal interest in you. If possible, ask the staff what they like the most about working there and what the biggest complaints tend to be from their perspective and from a resident's perspective. Ask them what the residents enjoy the most about living there. If they can't answer your questions transparently, that tells you what it is like when you as a family member are not there.

It was a stunning revelation. All of these people worked there, but no one seemed to care that the residents were just existing there, occupancy was in decline, and the business was losing money every month.

Any efforts to please the residents seemed pedestrian to me, as only a few dedicated and self-motivated caregivers went the extra mile.

Seemed to me, though, that everyone should be worried that the census (number of residents in the building and the key to all the business metrics) was so low that they were at risk of losing their jobs.

By keeping my ears open and my mouth shut, I learned that the staff intentionally failed to perform well on tours and looked for opportunities to deliberately dissuade people from joining the community.

I could hardly believe it. Why would they do such a thing? Why? Because, as someone let slip, "The better we do at marketing, the more residents, the more work. We are not going to get more help or pay, so who needs that?"

I was blown away.

Truth was, it started at the top. The administrator, who was playing card games at her desk during work hours, was asleep at the wheel.

After over half a year of watching this and reporting to my father, one day a crisis came up that threatened to turn our 130-apartment community into a health hazard for our residents and into bankruptcy for the family business.

Turns out, we literally sprang a leak: the water heater had ceased working and was flooding the basement. To top it off, Georgette's system of favoritism with the caregivers had caused massive disruption to morale within the department, and half of the caregiver staff was at war with the other half, with both sides threatening to walk out, potentially leaving us in a nightmare situation.

I went into Georgette's office and asked her what she was going to do. She seemed paralyzed. When I pushed it, she said it would blow over, that staff would not leave and that the leak was not so bad. Not only had she not left the office to go see it, she was trying to convince me that it would all just go away. She did not care.

I finally lost my patience. I was livid. I told her that her management of the care of our residents and the business was completely unacceptable.

With that, she snapped out of her coma and turned to me with a grin like a Cheshire cat. She told me I had no idea what I was doing or what I was talking about, and that just because "Daddy" sent me here did not mean I knew more than her and her twenty years of experience.

"You're fired, Georgette." It came out before I knew what I had even said. I told her she was terrible at her job and did not care about the residents, their families, or the staff. Or even us. She said that I could not fire her, that only my father could. I called a maintenance guy, Luis, to bring boxes, and we put her belongings in, gave her a check, and escorted her out the door.

As I walked back into the building a few minutes later, to my surprise the entire staff was now at the front, standing there frozen. I went into Georgette's former office to call headquarters and asked Luis to call water heater repair companies.

I closed the door. When my father got on the phone, I said, "Dad, I fired Georgette. I had no choice. She turned the caregiver staff against each other; half are about to walk out. We have a flood in the basement, and she was playing computer games and did not give a darn. I fired her, I asked Luis to call people to fix the boiler, and we need a new administrator."

"Good, David," he said.

"It was pretty hard to fire someone for the first time, but she deserved it, and now we can get someone good."

"David," he said. "Congratulations, you are the new administrator."

What had I done?

Chapter 4
LONG-DISTANCE LOVE

When I was a young child, my favorite person in the whole world, other than my mom, was my grandmother. I cherished her. Most of my friends had four grandparents. I only had one, my mother's mother, Gizella. Both of my father's parents, Ephraim and Yehudit, and my mother's father, Hillel, had been brutally murdered in World War II. She was, therefore, the only grandparent I had ever met, but she was enough to fill my heart completely.

My grandma had the warmest smile, the sweetest eyes, and a shock of white hair that she refused to color. She lived on the other side of the world from my home in Los Angeles. Every summer when I was small, my mother and I would fly to Israel and live with her for a few hot sweltering months in her tiny apartment in Tel Aviv, just blocks from the beach.

She spoke almost no English. We communicated through a cloudy combination of English, Hebrew, Romanian, Hungarian, and body language. I had little to no idea what she was ever talking about, but she was always so happy to see me and so warm and huggy that it never mattered.

We had a language all our own. It involved playing games, taking walks together, going to the market, and fumbling through a story here and there. She also used to play tarot cards. I found some of the cards to be a little scary as a child. She would play the cards and speak out loud in Hungarian or Romanian as if I understood each word. If I got a bad card, her eyebrows would rise, and she would make a face like it was an unwelcome prediction of the future. She would then pretend to spit on it to "wipe away" any bad karma and then gently caress my cheek and smile to reassure me that all was going to be okay.

Sometimes she would read aloud to put me to sleep. My lack of understanding of her words rocked me into a deep slumber every time.

Grandparents, I later learned, have the best of both worlds—all the fun with none of the discipline. When they've reached their limit, they hand the kid back. She never handed me back.

I looked forward all year to living with my grandmother. We'd wake up to the smell of Nescafe coffee, vegetables, bread, and eggs. I would walk a few blocks to the beach and spend most of the day there for relief from the summer heat. Usually my mother came, but sometimes I went alone.

When it was past lunchtime, and the hottest part of the day approached, I would walk back, and we would have lunch and a nap. They called it a siesta.

Lunch was almost always the same. Schnitzel. You beat eggs and add oil, salt, and pepper and coat the meat, usually chicken, with the egg mixture, then roll it in breadcrumbs and toss it into a skillet to fry until golden brown. I watched her do it a thousand times. If I close my eyes, I can still smell the deliciousness.

After we ate, Grandma would scrape up the leftovers, and my favorite moment of the day would finally arrive. She lived on the third floor of an apartment building, and at the end of the meal, she would cut up the remaining schnitzel into tiny pieces and open the window to the side of the building. There, she and I would make a kissing sound over and over.

To my delight, every time we did this, twenty to forty cats would appear below her window, three stories down, meowing and singing to her to throw the delicious food down. We did this together every day, and although it is a simple act, it was absolutely magical to me. We would laugh and smile at them, and at the end, she would tell them something, which I think was that we would see them all again tomorrow.

Another daily ritual involved watermelon. Watermelon was the best thing you could ask for on a hot summer day. The country was young and unsophisticated, so it seemed normal to me to hear the clack-clack of horseshoes on street pavement. When you heard that sound, it meant the watermelon man was in his horse-drawn cart coming down the middle of the street. He would yell, "*Avatiach!*" which means watermelon in Hebrew.

When we heard that, we did not have much time. Grandma would run for her purse and give me some change. Then I would run down three flights of stairs and try to catch the horse-drawn carriage full of watermelon before he passed my street. I would pick out the biggest melon I could afford, pay the man, and try to carry it upstairs. Problem was, I was little, and the melons were big. Most days I won and got the melon upstairs. A few times, however, I would pick one that was simply too big, and the staircase ended up getting the melon. I would go to Grandma with tears in my eyes, and she would walk back with me to help clean it up and salvage what she could.

Years later, as a teenager studying abroad, I would get one weekend off a month. Any Friday I had off, no matter where I was spending the weekend, I would take the long bus ride to Tel Aviv and buy flowers to bring to Grandma. She always said I should not spend what little money I had on flowers, but the way her face lit up when she opened the door and saw the flowers was the happiest moment of my month.

No, that is not true. It was the second happiest moment. The happiest was when, after she put the flowers in a vase, she would turn toward the kitchen, and before I knew it, the schnitzel had hit the pan.

Eventually, I moved back to the United States, and even though Grandma came to live with us now and again, she preferred to live in in her own home in Israel. She refused to stay with us, saying that she wanted to be independent and that was her place in the world. She was inflexible. This was especially difficult for my mother, who worried constantly about her living alone.

One day I came home from school and found my father consoling my mother, who was hysterically crying. My father pulled me aside and told me that Grandma had passed away in her sleep. In our culture, this is a sign of a righteous person blessed from above to not suffer.

I felt like a building had fallen on me. For my family and me, and especially my mother, the joy of life was gone for quite a long time.

Nearly thirty years later, when my father was fighting illness himself and close to the end, he told me there was something I needed to know. He told me that Grandma had actually not passed away in her sleep. In fact, she had fallen in her home, alone, and had gotten hurt. No one was around to help her. She was unable to reach the telephone and too far out of range for anyone to hear her likely distress calls. She was so independent that no one immediately worried. She had apparently been alive for at least a day or two on the floor before one of her sons got worried and went over. He found her dead on the floor.

I listened and tried to stay composed. I failed. I got up and stormed out of the Cedars-Sinai chemo lounge we were in, infuriated that no one had told me the truth, that she had suffered and met her end that way, that she was allowed to live in such an unsafe situation because no one wanted to fight with her about the dangers of being alone and isolated at her age.

The thought of my beloved grandmother on the floor, in pain, suffering, and dying alone overwhelmed me with an anger and sadness I had never felt and have never recovered from completely. Even thinking about it today brings tears to my eyes.

When I worked in senior living, people came for tours all the time to see what we offered. They would tour and then say they needed to think about it or see other places. After a while it was easy to see who was serious and who was simply putting their toe in the water.

I would wait a week or month and follow up with all inquiry tours by phone. When the daughter or son would hear my voice and get choked up, I knew what was coming. The adult child had submitted to the parent's will and had not insisted on the move, only to find Mom dead on the floor or Dad injured in the shower. I'd hear that the parent had likely been there for days and suffered horribly and unnecessarily, and that the child's pain and guilt were overwhelming.

"If only Mom had made the move, she would not only have been happier, but she likely would be alive today."

All I could do was try to offer comfort.

Whenever I received a call from a family regretting that they never made the move, no matter what time of day, after I had checked that all in the community was okay, I would pack up, get in my car, drive the hour home, crawl into bed, and try to imagine going back in time to come to my grandma's rescue.

Chapter 5
GOING ROGUE

I have been going rogue my whole life. I have always been on the road less traveled. I don't think I chose it; I think it chose me.

When what is before me makes no sense or seems inherently wrong, I have felt a gravitational pull toward an alternative path that may or may not exist. In college, my psychology professor handed out a list of quotes and asked us to pick the quote that most closely connected to our "spirit." One quote jumped off the page:

"There are those who look at things the way they are and ask *why?*" I dream of things that never were, and ask *why not?*"—Robert F. Kennedy.

As I sat in the administrator's office as the new de facto leader of this community, that quote rang in my ears. If I was going to do this, I was going to do it *my* way, not the way everyone else was doing it—and failing. My place, and senior living as a whole, could be fixed. If we organically created solutions and did not force-feed corporate control and instead worked together, we could be successful. The model would evolve, and success would be born. This would require a total reboot so that the experiences of the resident and of the family would become the opposite of their current experiences.

In order to do that, I would need to focus on the most important element of the operations, and the one that everyone viewed as the biggest negative. The staff was the key to everything. By developing, empowering, and nurturing the staff to use their judgment and think problems out (instead of the corporate concept of eliminating all independent thought), then 90 percent of my work would be done for me. This meant turning our staff—or our "paid enemies," as I once heard someone in the business call their employees—into our biggest advocates and problem solvers. This involved trusting them, and this concept would be a transformative change. By turning the staff into mini-mes, we could eliminate the mountain of time spent controlling them and instead allow them to function in a natural and optimistic way. We would replace fear with information. Replace authority with integrity. Bypass the industry systems, rules, and gatekeepers and go directly to the client for direction. Reject the "we know what is best for you" approach. Together we would unlock, inspire, and create a future that people actually thrive in, look forward to, and, dare I say, enjoy.

I had just fired Georgette, was sitting in her office, and clicked back into the fact that I was the new administrator. The good news was I had been an employee my whole life, so I knew how they thought. The bad news was I had no idea what I was about to do. I figured I would go check the boiler, calm everyone down, keep the caregivers from walking out, and look like I was not crapping in my pants.

I walked out to get some fresh air, but in the waiting room adjacent to the office stood nearly the entire staff waiting for me. So much for the not crapping in my pants.

As I gazed into their concerned faces, it was impossible not to feel their tension and fear. Nothing had prepared me for this moment. I knew I only had one chance to win them over and about sixty seconds to do it. The room was stuffy and the air heavy. I had no time to think. I decided to go with honesty.

"Okay, everyone, so here is the deal. This is a good news/bad news situation. I just fired Georgette. She did not care about the residents, their families, you, or me. She had to go. We all deserve better. And the boiler is broken, and we have a flood downstairs that Luis is trying to deal with, and we have no hot water. Probably will not have hot water until tomorrow, and the residents and their families are going to be unhappy. So it is pretty simple. I am taking over as administrator starting now, and I need your help. Our seniors need your help right now. **The only reason any of us is here is because of them**. So we are going to work together and help each other, and we will figure it out. Tomorrow is going to be tough, but the good news is every day it will get better, and every day we will work together, and a month from now you will be happier. A year from now, we will all be doing better than ever, and Sunnycrest will be full with happy seniors, and you will be happy as well. But if you like Georgette, want to join Georgette, or want to work for someone like Georgette, this is not going to work, because I will be the opposite of her in every way. So I am telling you right here and right now if you want her here that is fine, but you should leave and you should leave right now. There is the door. Use it. I will pay you what you are owed and wish you well, but there is the door. If you liked the way things were going, you should go with her or just go. Now."

I held my breath and waited. No one moved. Everyone looked around, but no one moved an inch. "I am serious. Leave right now. But if you stay, you are a part of the future, with me, and things are going to be different starting right now. **Choose**."

No one moved. "All right then. It is almost dinner, so housekeeping, maintenance, and I are going downstairs to clean up the basement. Kitchen staff, get ready for dinner, and caregivers, take care of the residents the way you would want your parents taken care of."

With that, I stormed out like a general leading troops to battle. Truth was I hoped no one realized how scared I was, and I prayed that when I looked behind me I was not alone.

I turned around, and nearly everyone was right behind me. It was the start of a new world for me, and it felt like being dropped into a fighter jet in the middle of a dogfight with people shooting at you from all directions. That feeling only lasted about eighteen years.

Chapter 6
THE ABCs OF SENIOR LIVING

This chapter is devoted to helping you understand the choices and unusual terminology of senior living. Refer to this chapter anytime you feel confusion as to where you belong and what people are speaking about. I will explain the terms used, what they mean, and, finally, what they *really* mean.

Think of senior living as a ladder. I am going to present an extremely inappropriate way to think about it, but you will instantly understand and remember it, so deal with it.

Think about senior living as a ladder. The higher up on the ladder, the closer you are to dying. The lower on the ladder you are, the healthier you are and more able to take care of yourself and your needs. The higher on the ladder you are, the less independent you are, the more care you need, and the more fees you will likely be facing.

The senior who is still living at his or her home is the first rung on the ladder. This is either the elder who is alone or a couple whose children live elsewhere. They believe they want to age in place or tell you they plan to "die at home with their boots on" rather than live in a facility for one minute. They inevitably get outside care to come in or live-in help at home, and stay in the familiar place but live in relative isolation.

One rung up from living in the original home is **fifty-five-and-over housing**. There was a time when fifty-five was considered elderly, but nowadays no one living in one of these communities is within twenty years of fifty-five. These places tend to be old two-story motels with a pool, lots of parking spaces, and some public areas. They

Spoiler Alert: The people who advocate or stick with this path are usually those adult children afraid of the difficult, complex, and inevitable reversal of roles between parent and child that often occurs, or they are marketers and others who profit from parents staying at home.

generally do not provide food or care. You live in a studio in a hotel without room service. The benefit is that you are not alone, and there are people close by who will know if you are not okay. The negatives are that you do not have daily living services, food is not provided, and there is no activity or safety net other than other residents or the person at the desk, who hopefully keeps an eye on you. These places are very popular for one reason: they are dirt cheap. Government agencies keep rates low, and seniors generally love to spend as little money as possible.

The next rung up is **independent living** (IL). IL is the opposite of what it says it is. There is nothing independent about independent living, but the senior-living industry tries to play with your fears, so this is what it is titled.

TIP: In California, an Independent Living community is governed by Title 22 of the Health and Safety Code. Title 22 provides the rules and regulations, and if you ask a marketing person or an executive director what their history of compliance is with Title 22 of the Health and Safety Code, they will probably need a change of underwear because they will be so shocked you know that. After they recover, you could and should ask to see a copy of their last state licensing visit. It is supposed to be posted publicly, and it lists everything found during the last visit. This document will tell you more than a thousand brochures or marketing e-mails. If they have not posted it, you should wonder why, since they know they must. If they refuse to give it to you, walk out.

In brochures and marketing materials, some communities portray their seniors participating in ballroom dancing, or eating like they are in Monte Carlo about to play baccarat, or driving a convertible one hundred miles an hour with their hair on fire. It is all nonsense. IL means we, the community, generally provide three meals a day in a dining room at set times, do some form of daily housekeeping, fix anything that is wrong with your apartment (or unit, as industry people like to call it), as well as provide entertainment, activities, and limited transportation. In other words, all you have to do is keep breathing and show up to eat and go places, and we do everything for you.

Sounds very independent, doesn't it? One key factor to recognize is that most IL apartments do not have kitchens. Most seniors have cooked and cleaned their whole lives and have had enough of it. Going to the market, dragging groceries to the car, carrying them inside, putting them away, cooking, and cleaning up the mess has lost much of its appeal for most older people. And cooking often involves some degree of danger, like leaving the stove on or putting something in the microwave that should not go in there or burning things. These real concerns are a burden to seniors and their sometimes-fearful families.

The costs of senior living start to bump up in IL. Generally, IL costs between $2,000 and $4,000 a month on average for a studio or a suite. A suite would naturally cost more because it includes a separate bedroom instead of just a studio with a bed in it. Each unit has a private bathroom, and you live by yourself. In the old days, most residents had a shared apartment in which two people lived, but each had his or her own bed or bedroom. This nursing home model was useful when no one wanted to move in, and you were dying for residents and asking them to pay, so they would play on the "better not to be alone" concerns. But the industry eventually figured out that it is better (i.e., more profitable) to have a single person paying full price rather than two paying the price of one.

In most cases, this fee is a bargain. All of your expenses, except your phone, are included in that fee. You do not pay for water, power, food, entertainment, transportation, repairs, or cleaning services. Unless your home is paid off, which is the case with many, it makes a pretty compelling case simply on a financial basis. However, most in the senior-living industry fail to make this honest and logical case intelligently, instead relying on emotional manipulation sales techniques.

The next rung up is **assisted living** (AL), the older sibling to IL. They are in the same family, and AL is also governed by Title 22. AL means that you have all the same stuff one gets in IL, but for an additional fee, staff may assist you with a higher level of personal care, such as medication management and distribution, perhaps assistance with bathing and/or dressing, and other personal matters. These services generate new fees, usually called "care" or "services." This is where the prices start to get serious. Care elements usually go for a minimum of several hundred dollars a month, and someone who needs some care often needs a lot. The less independent you become, the more services you need. Compared to what a nursing home costs, or even home care, the fees are quite reasonable, and the care comes to you. You also deal with the same staff as opposed to the frequent turnover of a home health company.

Medication management, which is the most common service people want, costs around $300/month. They order, organize, and dole out medication per the physician's instructions at the time of the order. The staff must ensure that the pills are taken according to the prescription, and this is generally a big relief to both the family and the residents. Medication errors are potentially dangerous, and seniors have been known to forget to take their pills. Other available services range in action and pricing, and full packages of care can top out between $1,500 and $2,000.

Most communities use the "level" or the "point" system to determine fees. In the level system, the staff decides that you are on a certain level and have to pay for that tier of services. The problem is that most people do not need all of the services at that level yet have to pay for them. The point system, on the other hand, tracks how many actions are performed by a staff member, assigns a point to the action, and you pay the points. The downside here is that you do not always know how many points are being generated, so the fee at the end of the month may come as a shock and blow your budget. Since the actions have already occurred, you cannot argue that you should not have to pay for them, and you are relying on the community to honestly and accurately bill you. No conflict there…

Yes, I was being sarcastic. At the community I ran, I had an a la carte system in which you paid only for what you wanted. You could pick and choose; we did not pick for you. This system cut down on runaway fees and the subsequent sticker shock. But the senior-living industry, for some reason, prefers their systems to mine. When you run a community and come to know the residents and their family members personally, and they know you, a heightened level of honesty exists because they become like family. Instead, the senior-living industry keeps things corporate and at arm's length while giving the appearance of a sincere and family-oriented relationship. When you browse websites and brochures, see if any of them mention the word "family."

The next rung up the ladder is a **nursing home**. The key point to keep in mind is that nursing homes are medical facilities, whereas IL and AL are not. Nursing homes are staffed with nurses and certified nursing assistants (CNAs), and most IL and AL facilities are not. The ALs that have nurses employ them because it is a great marketing tool to attract new residents. A community is not required to have a nurse; we never had one, and it had no impact. In the broadest of terms, nursing homes are for sick people. IL and AL facilities are not. That is the main difference, along with the expense.

AL is now seen by many as the alternative to a nursing home, and ALs now do a lot of what nursing homes used to do. Some fear that ALs are becoming too medical and should have staffing ratios and more oversight like nursing homes. Nursing homes have certain standards, and treating AL like nursing homes would be an enormous error that would likely retard the benefits to seniors instead of enhancing them. Many in the industry are concerned that if a national standard was created, it would be the first step toward government control. While I agree that government tends to negatively impact industries it touches, a national standard is exactly what the industry needs.

Currently, the industry prefers to judge itself, and some believe the only metric it cares about is profit. There is no transparency, and the consumer often finds the journey before, during, and after the decision to "purchase" to be dark and somewhat scary. It need not be. **We should illuminate the path and make everything user friendly and clearly understandable.** This would revolutionize the senior-living industry, but major players in the industry financially benefit from the confusion and lack of information as it stands.

I truly believe a national standard could lift all boats, and that the marketplace will naturally reward the great and hurt the incompetent. But let us table that discussion for now. You are here to learn to navigate these choppy waters, and I am here to light the path with information and insight.

Hospitals are the next rung up the ladder as we get closer to God, or the end, or however you wish to think of it. I feel no need to explain hospitals; however, there is one level that fits into all of these rungs on the ladder and is relatively new: **hospice care**. Hospice care has emerged as a force, not only in terms of relieving pain and suffering due to end-stage illness but also as a serious business. One dirty little secret of SL is how many aggressive and immoral hospice agencies have popped up. Hospice is very important, and I have seen it work in a beautiful way, but I have also seen a small percentage of hospice agencies act in ways that are disgusting and extremely and exclusively profit driven. Do your homework here, as a great hospice agency can be an angel, but I have also seen the devil, and she was pushing hospice because it is a huge money-maker. I have seen and heard of hospice agents doing immoral things to sign up clients, including telling them and their family they have a terminal disease when in fact they do not. Tread lightly here.

So let us make this a little more real. Let's focus on a theoretical person we will call Myrtle. Myrtle is a lovely lady who raised her five children, has eleven grandchildren living in three states, saw her wonderful husband (who was in the navy) fall ill and pass away, and has been living at home alone for years with the kids coming by to help whenever possible. Myrtle can take care of herself and suffers mostly from loneliness. When her husband passed away, eventually the other couples they were friends with carried on without her. Some of her relatives passed away, and perhaps she is most connected with a club or her church or some other organization. However, depression, lack of proper nutrition, a fall or two, or issues with the house or with her medications have led the family to conclude she might no longer be okay to stay at home alone. Perhaps someone from the family moved in, or the family increased their visits, or a live-in assistant was hired, or outside care comes in for part of the day. In the end, Myrtle's life is empty, and all she has are memories. She has little to look forward to and no one to smile with. She is the perfect candidate for IL.

Myrtle moves into IL. She is initially hesitant but then meets someone from her church there, or finds a class she enjoys, or discovers the Internet through an activity. She blossoms. This scenario happens repeatedly if the community has their act together.

Years pass. Myrtle slows down and is having balance problems. The family is concerned she might fall in the shower. A daughter has been helping her bathe, but cannot be there consistently. Myrtle is also having eyesight issues now, and the family is concerned she might mix up her pills. Now is the time to engage the community in their AL services. Now, keep in mind most IL and AL facilities are in the same building. At Sunnycrest, it was perfect: we had IL and AL people living side by side, and the staff came to them as needed.

Unfortunately, because the industry stresses profit over resident happiness, when you need AL, most places move you to a different floor or building. This is very disruptive to the residents, who have their home set up just right, have their neighbors, and have memorized the path to and from the dining room so they could do it in their sleep. If it were me, I would prefer a community that did not move Mom or Dad for staffing efficiency. The residents and their happiness must come first. In law, it is said that the omission of an act is itself an act. In SL, the omission is the failure to put the resident's needs ahead of the community's.

If Myrtle gets ill, breaks a hip, or has serious issues, a hospital is where she will go, and if she recovers, she will likely be sent to a nursing home or a rehabilitation facility until she is able to come home to the IL/AL community. Make no mistake, that will be home to her. It will be more than where her stuff is, where her friends are, and if the community has done things right, where she is loved and missed. You will know it is the right place if they visit her wherever she is to check on her and if, when she does come back, the staff and residents are waiting in the lobby to welcome her home. That is how we did it. That is how I would want it done for my family. That is the standard we should aspire to.

Chapter 7
INSIDER TOURING GUIDE AND SENIOR-LIVING SECRETS

Now that you know the ABCs of senior living, the next step is determining which community is the right fit for you or your loved ones. This chapter contains insider tips and tactics to use so that you shift the odds of long-term success dramatically in your favor. These tips, revealed myths, and rarely discussed suggestions provide insight that may be counterintuitive or shocking. Trust this playbook and the step-by-step process and you will be richly rewarded.

Welcome to the guide that senior-living providers don't want you to read

These insider tips will assist you in finding which level and which community is right for you. SL has become a complex and confusing maze designed to funnel you into certain communities that may or may not be the best fit. Choosing or being pushed to the wrong community could have a deep and significant impact. Many communities and referral agencies focus their efforts on marketing and profits instead of creating happy residents, with the assumption that you will not want to move again even if you are unhappy.

Did you ever walk into a community and see people asleep in the lobby or congregated comatose in front of a television? Or one that has *that smell*? Those are the facilities you want to avoid. This chapter will go much deeper. Arm yourself with this critical knowledge as part of your research process when calling and touring.

This step-by-step guide provides a clear road map to help you navigate through the noise and see past the glossy brochures. Whether you are looking for yourself or a loved one, the goal is the same: determine which option is right for you and choose the winner.

Ten insider tips (plus SL secrets) to give you the edge

1. **Surf before you walk.** Starting your search online before you hit the bricks is smart. Just remember that corporations spend massive amounts of money (from the rent of current tenants) on their websites and Internet advertising to get you on the phone speaking to their highly trained marketing agents. Check out what *customers* say about your potentials, not what they say about themselves. Sites like Yelp.com,

SeniorAdvisor.com and Caring.com give third-party opinions and are good starting points to see what actual clients have to say about the communities you are considering.

While anyone can post a single uncomplimentary Internet review, look for majority opinions. See *if* the community itself responded to a negative review and *how* it responded. A community that responds to comments in a professional and nondefensive way is a community that cares. Communities that ignore reviews and feedback are likely to ignore *you* once they have your money. Communities that respond now are likely to keep on caring.

2. The truth about "free" referral agencies. People stepping into this world are led to believe that referral agencies are selfless quasi-charity organizations with a personal touch and zero economic motives. While that is true for some, it is very not true for others. Most national referral agencies do little more than put your personal information into a database and send it to selected communities. Their criteria for choosing one community over another may not be what you think it is, or what it should be, which is finding the most appropriate home based on your personal and specific needs.

The truth is that some placement agencies use other questionable criteria, and virtually all of them are paid a sizable fee by a community if you move into it. Fees range from 50 to 100 percent of your first month's fees. Not exactly free or selfless.

Some privately encourage you on the phone (so there is no provable paper trail) to focus on a specific facility for reasons that may be questionable. We annually tested agencies, and year after year we explained that my "aunt" lived a few blocks between Sunnycrest and a nearby competitor and that I needed to stay within budget and within a mile of her current home. The referral agent said she had a perfect place for my "aunt" and sent me a list that fit my criteria. However, during subsequent phone calls, the agency pushed us to visit a huge corporate chain that was not only many miles from her doctors and church but in a different city entirely! It was the closest location of a certain megacorporation. When I pointed this out, the agent asked me, "You love your aunt, right?"

I said, "Of course I do."

"Then trust me," she said. "Send her to community X." Feel free to draw your own conclusions.

Having said that, excellent and reputable referral agencies do exist. Many give you personal attention and work to find the best place that fits your needs. You may be shocked to learn that most of the national referral agents you may speak with have never actually been in the buildings they are recommending. Ask the agent the last time they have been to the places they are recommending.

3. Narrow your list to three places. Review websites and speak to friends, doctors, and family about positive or negative experiences, with the goal of narrowing your tour list to three possibilities. Most people call the eight to ten closest places, ask basic questions, and choose five places to visit. That is a big mistake. The call is the most overrated element of this process. Why? Because the best places focus on the residents, not the marketing calls. As counterintuitive as it sounds, you might eliminate the right place simply because you were put on hold, or the key person was unavailable (likely helping an actual resident or family) versus the community that has marketing staff focused on generating new revenue from you. Keep that in mind when you call. Choose the three communities based on **location, price, and ownership**.

These are critical elements, so let us examine them individually:

- **Location:** Location is critical for several reasons. First, you want to be close to a respected hospital. The distance to travel to one in an emergency can make all the difference. Second, physicians tend to have offices near hospitals, so that makes routine care easier. Finally, you want to be surrounded by life: restaurants, shopping, coffee, a post office, and more, all within walking distance (even if you don't do much walking). Being stuck in an isolated building away from life and action is a huge negative that you may regret.

Don't play in traffic. Older people move slowly, thus seniors and traffic do not mix. Pick a community located off the beaten path. It's better, and likely safer, to be on a quiet street than on a congested street with traffic, dirt, and noise. Corporate America likes to place communities on the busiest streets possible for visibility and marketing reasons, but do you really want a facility right off the freeway? Neither would I. But at the same time, you don't want to be isolated. Choose a location that has useful places you can walk to within a block or two at the most. It is great to stroll and stay active. Having a coffee shop, post office, and restaurants within walking distance on a quiet street makes it fun and easy to go out as you please, allowing you or your family member to maintain your freedom and independence.

- **Price:** Pricing is a critical issue, so I am giving it triple coverage.

Biggest SL myth: you get what you pay for. One dirty little secret of SL is that many communities are **chains owned by giant corporations publicly traded on the stock market.** They serve their shareholders, who seek and expect maximum profits despite whatever imagery the glossy marketing package reflects. Learn which companies have stock tickers and realize their fees may include advertising for other communities, squeezed profits, boards of directors on salary (and/or with stock options), fancy headquarters, and other hefty corporate fat. Decide if that is the best use for your money.

Ask twice about price. Call and get specific prices before you visit. Be sure to look for hidden costs. Ask everyone to quote a price on the same thing; for example, the price for a one-bedroom unit with medication management. Then you will have a baseline point of comparison. Be wary if they refuse to give you a specific price over the phone, or if they give you prices in a confusing way, like costs per day (designed to confuse you and make their fees not look horrific). This area needs more transparency. I would eliminate any place that insists you must come in to get a quote or so they can evaluate your needs. They know the answer no matter what they say. If you can't get a straight answer, the company is not being transparent.

Know your budget. Decide on a realistic price range before your visit, allowing for assisted-living fees in the future. Keep in mind that you will most likely eliminate food costs, utilities (except phone), and cable (although some now pass the cost back to you). You'll eliminate repairs, appliance replacement, and many other emergency bills. Also, know that (here is dirty little secret number two) **nearly all communities have a 2 to 8 percent annual rent increase**. This information should be readily available to you from the marketing people. They are required by the state to have a state rate disclosure form. Get it. If they do not have it, there is a problem. Even with that annual increase, you'll likely discover that living in an SL community pencils out very favorably, and many have said they wished they had made the move sooner.

- **Ownership:** Anyone can have a beautiful building on a safe street, but that is just the beginning of what you should look for. Buildings are just materials. What counts are the staff and if the ownership cares about the residents and the staff inside. Do not underestimate the importance of pride of ownership. Caring, stable, and experienced owners who have stood the test of time are an absolute must. A third dirty little secret about SL is that communities frequently get bought and rebranded, and the people you dealt with today may not have been there a year ago, and may not be there tomorrow. Good staff get kicked "upstairs" to corporate, and you are left with what you are left with. The departure of the best people is the opposite of what you want as a resident or family member. No one talks about this, but it is common. This is another area in which being publicly traded may matter.

Sunnycrest, by contrast, had been owned and operated by the same family that built it nearly thirty years prior. Resident and employee happiness, safety, and longevity matter to a long-term owner. The executive director, executive chef, and maintenance supervisor had worked for me at Sunnycrest for a combined thirty-four years. Ask the executive director or marketer you are speaking with how long he or she has personally been at this specific location. The answer may shock you.

If possible, try to visit all locations in one day so the differences will be clear. Trust your eyes and nose and what you actually see, not the prepackaged narrative the staff have been trained to deliver. So how do you effectively tour a community and get to see what it is really all about and if it suits you? Here are a couple of tricks that give you the edge:

1. Arrive unannounced. Most people call and ask if they can come in at a certain time. Rookie mistake. When someone would call to tell us they were coming for a tour, I would issue a "Code Gold" to let all staff know in advance. They opened the windows or cooled down the model, they did extra clean up, and everyone smiled extra hard. Tours are given any time someone walks in, so once you have it narrowed down to three places, list them, starting from the one farthest from you, drive up, and walk in. You will see the real operations and how things are done normally. But even before you walk in, drive around the neighborhood and see if inviting shops exist within a block and how far the closest hospital is. Once you arrive, you should have several goals for the tour. Focus on apartments, care, food, and activities.

2. Bigger is better. Despite what you may have been told, apartment size matters. Most marketers try to minimize this because apartment sizes have been shrinking in newer buildings to jam in more rooms. The smaller the rooms, the more residents the chains can squeeze in, and the more profits they wring out. You may be told residents in small rooms will spend most waking hours out of their rooms in activities. Nice try. The truth is, even with a great selection of activities, most seniors spend considerable time in their apartments and do not want to live in a glorified closet. Most facilities then try to sell you on their community, not the apartment itself. Do you believe smaller is better? Neither does anyone else.

If you want your parent(s) to be happy, get them the biggest and brightest apartment you can afford—the one you would choose for yourself. If it is for a lady, seek out a walk-in closet. Men tend to care about the view. Each person is different, so find out what is really important, and do not compromise. Remember that corporate marketers are trained to anticipate your concerns and taught how to negate them and get you to agree that what you do not want is what you really want. Trust your instincts and do not allow anyone to tell you they know more than you what is best for your family member.

3. You will never be as young as you are today. The old version of SL is that it is where one goes to die. Today it is where seniors go to rejoin the living. People live longer, and their needs change. You might be independent today but next year need or want AL services. These services can add up, and there is also a little trick that may blindside you. Now is the time to understand the issues and choices.

TIP: Understand the care model of each community upfront. Many people focus on the cost of the apartment and ignore the care costs that they do not currently need, which is a mistake. As people age, their needs change, so consider the system and costs of each. Once you are in, you do not want to be surprised by costs, and, while most people prefer some degree of ignorance, that choice will not be a valid defense later on.

There are two basic models of care: the "level" system and the a la carte system. Most communities bundle their services and use either the point or level systems. This means you may wind up paying for services you neither need nor want that are included in the level. This is corporate America's favorite model because they charge you more and fatten up their profits. Look for a la carte pricing when you pick services, pay only for what you need, and maintain control.

Another key point you may not realize is that some communities will move you to a different wing, floor, or building if you need care. They may or may not explain that to you upfront. This is unsettling to residents, as their apartments are their homes, and to move just to cut staffing costs to the company is the opposite of what residents should expect. At Sunnycrest, we did not isolate people with care versus those without, or force them to change apartments for our convenience and economic benefit. It is a philosophical issue of respect to us.

4. Have a bite with open eyes. Show up during lunch, the busiest time of the day at any community, and ask to sit in the dining room and sample the food the residents are eating. If you do not like it, neither will your mom or dad. If your host hesitates to seat you or discourages you from eating, run. See if the staff in the front office is eating the same food as the residents. If there are no trays in the business office, they know something you don't know, so move on.

See if any of the chefs or cooks walk the dining room and speak to residents to accept compliments or feedback. If you see a chef walking the room, that community cares if people are happy and adapts to their needs. If you ask me, that place is the keeper.

5. Check for signs of intelligent life. Look for clues that the community and residents are living in the present. Are there flat-screen TVs? A Wii? Skype? There is nothing more satisfying than seeing a resident playing Wii bowling and getting a strike in a game with their grandkids.

TIP: Ask if they mind if you can randomly speak to residents, staff, and family members. This is the ultimate form of research and is very important. Speak to the residents away from staff so they can be candid. If the staff tries to pick the resident you speak with, take that as a bad sign. Tell the resident who you are and ask them how they are treated, how the food is, how the leadership is, and the like. Do not expect a perfect report card, but see if they give a mix of good and bad points, as that is more credible. Truth is, no place is perfect, but residents themselves are often the very best indicator of what you can expect.

TIP: Pick up the newsletter. This is the backbone of any community, and it should be a full calendar of interesting things to do. See what is on the calendar for that day and check it out. If you see staff wheeling in disengaged people to make it look good because they know you are there, it's time to move on.

6. Ask for the owner. Many giant corporations use the term "family" to feed the illusion that they are the opposite of what they actually are. To find out how a place is run, ask to meet the owner. If the owner is in corporate headquarters out of state, know that you will not be dealing with a "buck stops here" person in the future. If an issue arises, you're far more likely to get satisfaction from a local owner even if that person is not there daily. If there is an owner with boots on the ground who walks the building, attends events, knows staff, and eats the food, your odds of you or your loved one being happy go through the roof.

7. X-Factors. A few final important notes. If your loved one is a pet person, see if the community allows animals (and has an outdoor area for dogs to do their business), as not all facilities do.

See if they have a hospice waiver. Hospice allows you to stay in the apartment under certain circumstances until the end. Also, find out if the community holds religious services on-site, which can be critical for some. And, finally, **the best kept secret of all** is that the vast majority of people who move into SL have a much better life. They are well taken care of, have a safety net, eat well, are living with peers who understand them, and have social opportunities that provide a real life. For most, it is truly a better life and the right choice.

Chapter 8
THE HIDDEN REASON WHY

What was criminal law like? Why did you defend those people? Was it scary? Why did you really leave?

Those questions have been asked of me a thousand times, and I never shared the genuine truth. It was only after I left SL that I even discovered the ultimate truth myself. **I learned that I love to defend the underdog.**

"Why would you leave a law career to work in a family business?" My answer was always the same. I would explain that after nearly ten years in the law (including clerking during law school), the challenge had declined and I had become bored. I felt my family had done everything for me, and it was time to give back. But this was not the entire story.

The truth is that my passion was waning, my skin becoming so thick I was in danger of losing all feeling. When you are in that world and you see what I saw, you become hardened beyond recognition. Criminal law is incredibly exciting and intense and real. But it was also brutal and bloody, and at times, it filled me with total despair. So many broken lives and so much suffering, but what people did not realize is that I am not just speaking of the victims; I am also talking about defendants, the clients. One after the other, these often damaged and broken people would wash up upon my shore. As a deputy public defender, I did not choose my clients, and they did not choose me. Some administrator would play God and make the trains run on time by sending files and bodies within a bigger system that oozed out McJustice. I came in thinking I was going to help people and save the world one innocent person at a time. Boy, did I step in front of that train.

When I explained to people why I left the law, everyone understood the story and agreed with my logic. But the true reason I left was that I was unable to effectively and consistently help the underdogs. By the time they got to me, my clients were often far along the path of total denial or complete destruction. I was not saving people. I was not healing people. It was not due to lack of effort. It was the game itself. Very few clients that I got into rehab stayed straight. People I served well and for whom I got dismissals or reduced sentences or charges came back into the system. I would see them again and feel what I had done was meaningless. The only thing changing tuned out to be me. That was the landmine. My work felt like it was without deep satisfaction or meaning. No one was turning their lives around. I wanted to be part of the solution. Instead I was part of a giant machine. I was not seeing success stories. Families were being destroyed on both the victim side and the defendant side. The realization that virtually no one was being "rehabilitated"—or that the system had discarded the illusion it was there to change the direction of my clients' lives—was a devastating truth, and with the mass volume of cases dumped on the few and the proud, being a public defender was a completely unreasonable role. The volume and pressure, and all we had to deal with, resulted in the best attorneys doing a lot of blunt talk, damage control, and a lot of hand-holding, but there was virtually no healing, brilliance, or happiness for anyone. It was a daily train wreck, and I was sitting in the engine room watching, unable to do much to change the massive system.

I won many cases that I felt I should not have won, and I lost a lot of cases I felt I should have won. Truth be told, the victims do not get what they need, and the defendants usually either get more or less punishment than they deserve (for unjustified reasons). When I got in my car to go home at night, I felt an emptiness that I could not fill. I started to fill it in ways that were not good for me and saw others sliding down the same rabbit hole. I worked my behind off to be exceptional for my clients, who hated me much of the time and accused me of secretly working for the prosecutor. No one, except for our bosses and coworkers, appreciated what we did day in and day out to help these mostly lost and self-destructive people. I never did it for the appreciation, but respect and appreciation heal the soul. Work had ceased being satisfying. My goal in law was to help underdogs and damaged people. Suddenly I could not even help myself.

Changes needed to be made, and because I am a man of action, I began to make them. I tried not to take things so personally and not to bring things home. I was now dating seriously for the first time in my life, and I compartmentalized work. I had also been advised that I was being passed over for another promotion and was being transferred to a court an hour farther from home—the booby prize for willingly taking the hardest cases and stepping up for the difficult clients no one else wanted. It was demoralizing. Things brightened when my girlfriend and I decided to get married.

Soon after, my father surprised me in court one day. I had a case in the Santa Monica courthouse finishing a third-strike murder trial. My client was a Latino gang member who had allegedly cut the throat of a fellow gang member during a party. The victim was found dead on the sidewalk, his throat cut from ear to ear. A trail of blood ran from the victim, and when the police arrived, they literally walked the blood trail from the victim straight up to the apartment building, up the stairs, into his apartment, where they found my client in the bathroom with a bucket of water cleaning a bloody knife. When they arrested him, he allegedly made an un-Mirandized comment that he was going to "get off like O. J."

This kind of murder happens all the time, but no one cares. The news carries stories about certain crimes with certain elements, but murders such as this flow through the system, and no one blinks an eye. It was my first murder case, and I took it seriously. Months and months of work led to this trial, and everyone (including my supervisor) let me know that no one would or could win this case, but I tried like hell anyway.

As I stood up to do the closing argument I had practiced a thousand times, the door to the courtroom opened. I turned to see my father walk in. He had never wanted me to go into criminal law. I think in the ten years I was involved in criminal law, he had come to court to see me once. I stopped as he sat down in the back of the courtroom. I suddenly was full of fear that someone must have died, and he was there to tell me. But then he smiled and nodded like I should go on and that everything was fine. Shaking off the surprise, I turned around, nodded at the judge, clicked back into trial mode, and gave a great ninety-minute closing argument with no notes. My client, who acted like he hated me because I was white and he considered me part of "the system," had refused to talk to me for many months. He would not cooperate, discuss the case, discuss his side of it, provide names of one helpful witness, or help me in any way. One could almost believe that he wanted to be convicted so he could return to the only world that made sense to him—prison life. How sad is that? His family would later reinforce this point, telling me he was "mentally institutionalized," and they worried that perhaps he did this, if he did, because he could not handle being "out" in the world.

He did not speak to me at all during the trial, but that did not make me try less hard or have fewer fights as I passionately defended him. I gave a great closing. As I left the podium, I snuck a look at my father. He seemed in shock. His little boy was clearly neither. It was a transformative moment for a father and son. As I sat down, my client leaned over, smiled, and whispered to me something like, "Yo, homes, you almost convinced me I did not do it." I was never sure if that was what he said, and I might have not heard him correctly. Perhaps I heard what I wanted to hear. I did not ask because, frankly, I did not want to know the truth, and I still do not.

You still want to know why I left the law? I left because it was a life of daily sadness in which no one won, there were just degrees of losing, and for every person I helped, there were a hundred the tsunami washed away. I could not take it. I would see their faces and know so few had a real chance of joy, and there was little I could do about it. It began to suffocate me. I never cared about the recognition, glory, or promotions. I just wanted to do the right thing and help people and—yes, I knew it was naïve—to make the world better. I learned I could do neither. So when, after my closing, my father asked me to leave law and join him to work in senior living helping older people, considering my history and my path, it seemed like a perfect solution.

That is why I left. I also left because I did not want my wife living with someone consumed by murder trials, autopsy photos, and endless despair. I had to save myself.

I came to see senior living as the exact opposite of criminal law.

Seniors were the exact opposite of the people I worked with in law. The seniors *wanted* my help, *needed* my leadership, and appreciated anyone who would sit and listen to them, let alone be devoted to their happiness. It gave me a chance to go from mentally being a prison guard to being Willy Wonka at the Happiness Factory. Senior living saved me.

Chapter 9
#OLDLIVESMATTER

I grew up in a European family surrounded by extended family with whom holidays and important events were unquestionably spent together. At the dinners, the elder leaders would often say a few (or endless) words, and everyone followed a certain code of hierarchy. Everyone knew their place. The respected elders were on top, and the young members of the family were at the bottom and expected to keep their ears open and their mouths closed. The young knew nothing and were reminded at every turn.

This was the way of the world, as it had been forever, with the old teaching and sharing pearls of wisdom with the young to ensure survival of the line, much as it is in the animal kingdom.

That has all changed now. **Youth now rules.** The online world is ruled by young people. New has replaced proven. Different has replaced trusted. People today reject everything their parents did and used, and want everything customized to them and have even altered the basics of business (often for the better) in our new, unchained, "shared economy" business models. Take

Uber and Airbnb, for example. The base assumption is that everything they inherited is old and antiquated, and the world has been waiting for their brilliance to make it better, smarter, and fresher. The past needs to be flushed.

Youth, and most especially youthful beauty, has replaced wisdom and experience in our value system. How much money is spent on advertising products to stay young, delay aging, avoid wrinkles, tighten skin, lift saggy parts, or hide imperfections? It is like getting old is now a sin. Next time you are leafing through a magazine, count the number of seniors in clothing, makeup, and other such ads. The numbers will add up to zero. Think that is by accident? No, we have made a choice.

We have, as a society, put up a wall between the young and the old, and the old are the ones behind the gray glass. Old people no longer matter to society. Let me peel back the curtain and reveal how this historically sound and proven system has been hacked, disrupted, and turned upside down.

There is a universally accepted lie about SL, and it is the basis of what you think and believe. **The lie is that living at home—aging in place—is better than living in a community.** This is unilaterally accepted by society, but it is completely false, and I will explain why. What is most fascinating and revealing is the reason for the assumption held by nearly all of society (hence the 90 percent). The true source of this illusion is not experience, studies, or fact. It is a combination of two elements. One is how we, as a society, think of seniors and aging, and the second element is pure, toxic, misplaced guilt. Allow me to explain.

For as long as you have lived, you have been exposed to cringe-worthy images and stories about SL: what it is, what type of people live there, and what happens there. If you scour your memory, virtually nothing will come to mind. But that does not mean it is not there or that your mind has not been polluted and conditioned to believe SL is horrible and sad. It is, in truth, neither.

This is one of the key areas of failure by the SL industry. They do not address it in a meaningful way, or in any way at all. They hold their breaths and likely have crisis management plans should a rare bad story appear on the news, and they spend their time having meetings, attending conferences, and handing out awards and praise, congratulating each other on breakthroughs and innovation that reflect that they are the true leaders of this space.

The problem is that despite the waterfall of press releases, marketing e-mails, amazingly titled conferences, numerous webinars, expensive commercials, and more expensive celebrity endorsers, SL has been stuck at the 10 percent penetration rate and still is seen as the last resort. Why?

What is the source of this negative narrative? The unfortunate, hard truth is that despite our collective intellect and claims otherwise, we believe what we see, and what we see are movies, TV shows, cartoons, and imagery that portray seniors as weak, feeble, unintelligent, sour, needy people that no one wants to deal with or be around. **We consistently diminish and devalue seniors in our society.** Full stop.

Think of elderly people in television. Who comes to mind?

No one immediately, I would bet. If someone does come to mind, I wonder if it is in a negative way. There are more seniors around now than ever in the history of man. How many senior stars are currently on TV shows? Are they reflected in movies, in our media? Absolutely not.

Let's dig deeper. Think harder. Maybe you thought of *The Golden Girls*. That was a 1980s show. *Matlock*? Again, 1980s. Seniors are mainly portrayed in comedy shows as senile, bothersome, or stuck in time. They are fodder for jokes and ridicule.

Who is the most famous elderly animated character of the past twenty years? That would be Abraham

Jedediah "Abe" Simpson of *The Simpsons*. Let me make an example of him. You have seen his character and laughed like we all have. But is there more to it than meets the eye? Let us take a moment to look at this character a little deeper to see whom we have been laughing so hard at all these years.

Abe Simpson is a World War II vet and retired farmer who was sent by his family to the Springfield Retirement Castle. He is known for his long, incoherent stories and for his senility. In the show, Abe is treated as a child, mocked for his failing memory, ridiculed for falling asleep at inappropriate times, detested for long rambling stories no one wants to hear, and is left behind at every opportunity. He is a bitter, angry, lonely, and critical person. He is the exact opposite of the wise elder in the traditional grandfather role in the family hierarchy.

To sum it up, according to his Wikipedia page, "The Simpson family tries their best to avoid any unnecessary contact with Grandpa."

What does this say, and why is that such an easily accepted character? **Where is the "Old Lives Matter" movement?** It does not exist. Why? Because no one speaks for seniors. So I will pick up that flag and run with it. We devalue seniors on nearly all levels. They are viewed as noncontributing, miserly, difficult, and useless elements who have outlived their expiration dates.

Want more examples? In the animated movie *Up*, a man places hundreds of balloons on his house to float into space rather than move into a retirement home. This sad movie taught audiences just how far a cranky old man will go to stay at home and out of a senior-living community.

Ever see *Happy Gilmore*? Happy's grandmother owes the IRS big money, and her house is being seized. Gilmore has ninety days to come up with the cash or the house will be auctioned off. Grandma is forced to move into a retirement home until Happy produces the funds.

Upon arrival at the home, they are greeted by Hal, the assisted-living director. After Happy leaves, Grandma asks the seemingly kind Hal for a glass of warm milk, as it helps her sleep. Hal, who was the perfect professional in front of her family, replies, "You can have a warm glass of shut the hell up. You will go to sleep, or I will put you to sleep. Check out the name tag. You're in my world now, Grandma." Hal turns out to be a sadistic sicko. I recall watching it in the theater hooting and howling with laughter with everyone else. Years later, I watched it again, and when I saw this scene, I felt ill.

Remember *Seinfeld*? George Costanza's father Frank hated life so much he screamed, "Serenity now!" wishing he were dead.

Think this treatment is a thing of the past? I was on Instagram recently and clicked on a few suggested humor accounts. One of the first pictures I saw was three old shoeless buddies walking on the beach. The first one said, "It's windy today!" The second one said, "No, it's Thursday!" The third said, "So am I! Let's have a beer!"

Another showed two old ladies holding electronics. One says, "I've been calling you all day!" The other points to the device in her friend's hand and says, "That's a calculator."

Another shows an old lady with glasses driving a car with her terrified dog next to her, and the lady says, "All these damn deer on the highway!" To which the dog responds, "Those are people, Margaret, and you're on the sidewalk."

When I searched on "aging," I found this post: On aging: "21 yrs—woo! 22 yrs—woo! 23 yrs—woo! 24 yrs—woo! 25 yrs—woo! 26 yrs—wait. 27 yrs—oh God. 28 yrs—please make it stop." At the time (I looked at this months ago), it had 13,296 comments and 60,852 "likes."

A final post has a shot of an older man and three older women smiling. The woman says, "I can't remember who I am." The next lady says, "I haven't seen my kids in ten years." The third says, "I just wanna die." The man says, "I shit myself."

I am fighting back against all of this with my own Instagram: **old_lives_matter**. Please follow me!

I went to see the animated movie *Pets* with my children. Before the flick, there was an unexpected, funny, animated short film featuring the "minion" characters from another movie. In the short film, these minions come across a senior-living home: "Fuzzy Memories Retirement Home." The bored elderly are portrayed falling asleep, having hearing-aid problems, or with their teeth falling out. That was last weekend.

Growing older is considered such a sin that it is sparking legal action in Hollywood, of all places. Many actors want an law against posting actors' ages online. A lawsuit was recently filed that targets a leading movie and television information website for ageism. Supporters state that they wish to prevent age discrimination, as many actors have complained that they are passed over time and time again for roles as they get older. Females say there is a double standard giving older women even fewer roles while they age. "By the time you're twenty-eight, you're expired, you're playing mommy roles," stated actress Zoe Saldana, now thirty-eight and female lead of the blockbuster film *Guardians of the Galaxy*. Expired? That does not sound good.

Sadly, I can go on and on. I dare you to watch *Happy Gilmore* and not cringe when that scene comes on. That is the exact fear so many people carry. Did they always have it, or did shows and movies like that implant it or heighten it? We will never know, but what we do know is that this fear is real, and the truth is the people I have met in this space, virtually without exception, have, on average, been the nicest, kindest, and sweetest people I have known in my life. They are in senior care because they cared for a loved one, and this was the natural progression. That is the narrative the senior-living industry should amplify, especially because it is completely factual.

When the Northridge earthquake hit in January of 1994, my father called me, checked on me, and then said to get ready, as he was going to pick me up. We were going to Sunnycrest. I was a deputy public defender at the time, and no one from the office was going in to work.

He explained that he was unable to get through on the phone and he was worried. We had to go down and see if the residents were okay and if there was any damage to the building. I told him we likely would have a bigger problem, that staff probably was not going to show up (like at my office). He said nothing.

When we pulled up, we were relieved to see the building was intact. We parked and walked in, wondering what we were going to find. As we entered, I saw the last thing in the world that I expected. The lobby of the building was full of working staff. They were caring for the residents, calming and reassuring them, saying they were all in it together.

I watched as they handed out water, held nervous people steady, and patiently answered questions, finding ways to make them smile despite the stress and fear.

I was impressed but confused. How did they mobilize so much staff in such a short time, with no phones? We said hello to everyone, and the staff and residents approached us and hugged and welcomed my father by name (they did not know me) until everyone had said hi and chatted. Then we went into the administrator's office for a report (but actually to calm her down). You might recall Georgette from earlier in the story.

My father's presence sent a wave of comfort and pride through the building. It reassured everyone and sent a strong message that resonates with me even today.

In her office, the adults chatted, and I stayed quiet. Finally, when they had finished, I asked the administrator how she had contacted so many staff members so quickly. She stared at me. My father smiled. I was confused.

"I did not call anyone. The phones are down," she explained.

This confused me more. "So how is everyone here?" I asked.

"They all just came in on their own," she said. I was still confused.

"They came because they care, David," my father explained. "These are the kind of people who work for us. They are just good people."

In other words, no one called them, and they actually left their homes and families, after making sure they were okay, and then left them to check on their beloved residents. This blew my mind. At my work, no one was going in. But these people showed up simply because they cared so much and so sincerely. My father also should get credit, because, somehow, when he arrived, it was as if General MacArthur had returned. I learned a lot about leadership that day, but I also learned how special and selfless those employees were, and I never forgot it.

That is what AL people are like for the most part in my personal experience. Most of the year, SL is quietly chugging along solving problems, generally filling lives with joy, entertainment, nutrition, and care. Occasionally, an idiot does demented things that make headlines. Truth is, SL is probably overall much safer than living the outside world all alone.

But the senior-living machine does not show this face to the world, and that is a mystery to me. People are treated better, likely safer, and the employees are wonderful and occasionally angelic people.

Why has the media portrayed old people and AL so inaccurately and so horribly? I recall watching *All in the Family* as a child in the 1970s. The family patriarch, Archie Bunker, was created by Norman Lear. In 1999, *TV Guide* ranked Archie Bunker number five on its "50 Greatest TV Characters of All Time."

Archie was an old, white-haired, blue-collar man—a nonmalicious idiot and a "lovable bigot" who knew nothing and was constantly arguing politics with his young, liberal son-in-law, Mike. I recall laughing at Archie with my family and snickering at his stupidity. Little did I know that the devaluing and compartmentalizing of older people as powerful yet stupid, untrustworthy, and out of touch was happening before my eyes and without my knowledge. The seeds of what we see today were planted all the way back then, and perhaps intentionally, by the politically progressive Lear.

Just a couple of months ago, I heard that Lear—now in his nineties and producer of the hits *Sanford and Son*, *One Day at a Time*, *The Jeffersons*, and *Good Times*— was complaining that no one would listen to his idea for a new show about old people. The title of the show, which would be set in an AL community, was *Guess Who Just Died?* Seems as though younger people running things now do not want to listen to him and are dismissive of what this old white guy has to say.

Kind of ironic, Mr. Lear, don't you think?

Chapter 10
DRAGON SENIORS

I did not want to write this chapter. I knew from the beginning that I would reach this crossroads and realize I would not be fulfilling my duty and promise to help and be honest with you without it.

However, if we are truly going to peek behind the Gray Curtain, we need to go to its darkest corner. Until now, we have discussed the kind, sweet, and gentle senior. The kind who raised the family on nickels and dimes and smiles. The kind who fought and risked life and limb on the beaches of Normandy on D-Day. The kind who sit on park benches and smile at you.

But there is another kind of senior.

This senior is only spoken about in hushed tones and only to the closest family and friends. They are the impossible-to-deal-with elderly persons who know all the tricks of manipulation and guilt. They are the **Dragon Seniors**.

This strain of senior is on a level all its own. They not only have PhDs in making you feel horrible, they have written the course material. The game is simple: they want/need you to be at their beck and call and jump when they say jump, just as you did when you were a child. And what they want is not usually about health or safety, it is about keeping you on a string. The source of this behavior is not evil or nastiness; these seniors are usually repeating how they were raised, or they fear losing control. Or both.

The problem is that the antidote—love and attention—only makes it worse. The Dragon Senior's target is most often the daughter(s), and usually the eldest. Sometimes the eldest has baggage or indifference that results in a rejection of the mother; and sometimes it is a son who gets caught in the web. The daughter makes her mother the priority, arranging her life around the needs of the mother. I have yet to meet a Dragon Father. I sense they exist, but the next one I meet will be the first one.

Dragon Seniors make the family and/or community feel that they are suffering, that no one cares, that they are being abandoned or ignored, and possibly even on the verge of a total collapse that may include death. They know that, one day, this prediction will be right and that you know this as well. That is the big hammer, and it is surprising how often some use it. The senior is never content for long, no matter what, and the guilt and shame piled on the recipient is suffocating and often comes out sideways in ways they do not control.

Recently I went to an amazing concert. Maybe one of the best I have ever seen in my life, which is saying something. The lovely couple we went with were in a great mood and happy as we had a preconcert dinner and journeyed to the Hollywood Bowl. During the delicious meal, the wife got a call, and a look of serious sadness enveloped her face. She got on the phone and said a few words in a dire tone like someone who did not want to wake up a baby. The couple shared some beleaguered glances at each other, and the dinner continued, but the tone had changed. Later, during the concert, she got a text. Her face turned troubled, and she walked away to take the call. She did not return.

As we were driving home, she got another call. The crisis was worse now from her tone of voice, and the traffic made the entire situation feel like a crisis. I could feel the nervous energy in the car. It ate us all up. When we finally got away from the traffic, and she made yet another call, I heard what the crisis was about. The mother was patiently waiting for her daughter to finish the concert and to come over to deal with this serious issue.

My friend's entire night was impacted by this. I could see in her eyes that she could not fully be present or enjoy the concert. Her whole evening, as well as her husband's, was ruined. The mood was sour.

Oh, and what was the crisis? Illness? No. Medication missing or severe pain? No. Strange sounds outside? An intruder? No.

The mother's remote control was not working.

There are certain hands-off subjects regarding seniors. I am aware that no one talks this openly about such sensitive and potentially explosive true matters. But if not now, then when? And if not me, who is going to do it?

I had seen this dynamic many times as executive director of Sunnycrest. A smart and sophisticated daughter would walk in and ask to meet me, and we would sit and chat. She would ask me all the basic questions in a rehearsed way and control and run our little meeting. When she reached the end of her questions or script, or run out of gas, I would ask a few questions designed to identify what type of daughter she was. Was she the type who had a Dragon Mom? Usually not, as they are very rare in senior living. Why? Because those Dragon Moms control those around them, to the extent they can, and would *never* allow even consideration of a move into an assisted-living community. They have orchestrated the lives of others to center around them, and living in a community where they are not the focus and where their family, specifically their daughter, are not waiting on them constantly is not an acceptable option. This dynamic is part of the reason so many seniors do not live in, or reap the benefits of, senior living. It breaks those chains.

I once did a tour for a daughter who was very impressed with the community, the staff, and the apartments. At the end of the tour, I asked her if she wanted to place a hold on the apartment she liked. She broke down in tears. She told me there was no way her mother would *ever* move in, but she was trying to convince her. The daughter explained that she and her husband had plans for an anniversary trip to Hawaii, just the two of them. The one obstacle? Her mother refused to go to any of the siblings' homes, temporarily stay elsewhere, or have a caregiver in the home, and she was essentially forcing them to cancel their special trip. She told me her husband made a not-so-veiled threat should she not find a solution to this dilemma, hence the visit. He had worked hard for this trip, and it was their anniversary, and he wanted her to prioritize him for once. I was not surprised she shared all of this. It was not the first time I had heard such stories. I asked her, while she had tears in her eyes, why she thought her mother was like this. She turned to me, tried to smile, and said, "Would you give up having a personal slave?"

I asked if she would consider bringing her mom to visit me so I could introduce myself and key staff to her. The daughter's rings, earrings, watch, and jewelry were worth more than my entire universe, so I knew money was not the issue. She said that her mother had actually been in the car the entire time, sitting in the front seat with the air conditioning on. She had refused to even walk in and take a look. I asked if I could go outside and say hello. She welcomed me to try.

I knocked on the car's window, where the eighty-ish well-dressed lady sat staring straight ahead. She saw me and looked away. I asked if she would roll down the window. She ignored me. She was having none of it. The daughter wiped her tears, apologized for wasting my time, got into the car, and drove away, never to be seen again.

Dragons come in all shapes and sizes. One rainy April day, my receptionist said there was a strange lady in the lobby who wanted to see me and would not leave. She told me the woman would only speak to me personally and had referred to me by name. I went out and saw a tiny ninety- to ninety-five-year-old lady sitting in the lobby. Drenched from the rain, with a puddle of water under her. She looked pathetic. I asked the receptionist to get some towels and ask the chef to send up some soup.

Once in my office, she spoke in soft and polite terms, her European accent slipping out now and again. She said that she was poor, that her husband had passed many years before, they had no children, and she had been "forced" into a horrible community where they treated her terribly, the food was inedible, and the other residents were all crazy. She told me she grew up in the same area of Europe where my parents did. She knew it by my last name. The towels and soup arrived, and she dropped everything when the soup came. The way she eagerly ate the soup broke my heart. I explained that her income was way below what we charged for a unit in our community, not to mention care, and that I could not give her such a huge price break, as that would not be fair to the other residents.

She broke down in tears and showed me her bank statement. Then she actually begged me. It was more than I could take. She asked me to think of her as my grandmother. She had found my Achilles' heel. We had finally turned the community around and had rented all the units except one. It was at the end of a long hall, far from the dining room, was unusually small and dark, and had a view of the parking lot.

I said that I would rent it to her for what she could afford. In return, she could never tell anyone I was giving her a break, and she would have to pay for additional care or services, as the staff cannot work for free. She agreed and explained that she did her medication and bathing and walking on her own and that she needed only a place to rest her head at night. She hugged me and thanked me and moved in a few days later. I was proud of myself and felt it was the right thing to do.

That illusion was shattered almost instantly. She moved in late the night before she was supposed to, apparently driven over by the owner of the last place she stayed. I found that odd. What owner would drive someone to their next location? Uh oh, what had I done? My spider sense tingled.

The staff then hit me with the news. Since the moment she moved in, she had been calling for unpaid care, "room service," and according to the staff, she was driving everyone crazy. I went to see her. She sat up on her bed and was watching TV. I asked her where she got the TV. She said she had told the staff I had authorized one to be removed from a model apartment for her. I told her I had said no such thing. She did not even take her eyes off the TV. I asked what was going on. She turned to me and said, "Sonny, here is the deal. I'm here now, and there is nothing you can do about it. State licensing requires that you attend to my needs, and if you do not, I will call them and explain how you are abusing a ninety-one-year-old woman with no family or friends, and you know how sympathetic I can be when I want to be. They will believe me over you, or I could call a TV station and tell them things, and you'll be out of business. So be a sweetie and close the door on your way out."

I explained to her that I was an attorney and was going to evict her. She had been down this road before and recited how the courts and state licensing would favor her at every step and that it would take months, and that we would never see a dollar from her. Now I knew why the previous owner had driven her here.

I had been duped. I walked back to my office, stunned. My naïve innocence was my downfall, and she had used guilt and lies to get the outcome she desired. There may have been no scales on her skin, no fire out of her mouth, but her reptilian ways were indisputable. She was my first, but not my last, Dragon Senior.

I called my father and asked what he would do. He said she was clearly not new at this and I should go back and ask her what she wanted. I did. She said she would leave if I gave her a certain amount of money. I did, and she did. It was disgusting.

Does SL work for the Dragon Senior? No, it does not. Unreasonable requests and limitless needs do not parallel how SL operates. Senior living is designed to do the grunt work that people have grown tired of doing. It provides a safety net for those otherwise alone, and as a bonus, it offers entertainment and social connectivity. It makes life better and gives people the social element that time and loss have stolen from them. It is not a replacement for unbalanced familial relationships, nor is it the parallel to the "it takes a village to raise a child" concept. It does not take a village to contribute to making a senior happy. Much of it has to do with the senior. A happy person from birth to seventy usually stays the same (although they slow down) and becomes a happy senior. Someone who has never been happy is not going to magically transform once life starts getting harder and the calendar changes.

In conclusion, I hated writing this chapter. I hated living it even more. If you are looking for the magic bullet as to how to deal with this, I have it, but I am not prepared to share it right here for one simple reason: no one I have given it to has used it. They end up feeling worse than before when they failed to find the strength to break the chains. If I ever do the speaking tour behind this book, I may go there, but not today. That is a book within itself. All I can say is that love and pain often go together, and I just hate that so many have felt relief when a parent has passed away instead of rejoicing in their lives.

To the extent that we can control our emotions and actions, it is the senior that must bear the weight of these results, and, frankly, there is a much better way. Few of the afflicted, however, ever take that path. This is, sadly, one of the hidden reasons seniors have been ostracized and marginalized by society. These stories are more common than you might think. I have found that almost all families have at least one. As uncomfortable as it is to be this honest, the truth is that it is the seniors themselves who are trapped in a cage of their own creation. They spend so much time and energy controlling others that they forget to live. A large number of people, especially women, are impacted by Dragon Seniors. It is the darkest and my least favorite piece of the senior puzzle.

Chapter 11
THE MOST IMPORTANT CONVERSATION

The single most important conversation you will have during this process will be with the executive director of the community. This may or may not be easy to achieve, but it is absolutely critical. He or she will likely try to pawn you off on a marketing director or any of the middle-management people with fancy job titles that mean nothing. Do not comply. They are blockers, pure and simple, designed to keep you away from the key person, the quarterback, the executive director.

The executive director (ED) is the brain of the entire operation, the final authority, and the ultimate decision-maker in-house. Establishing a personal connection with the ED is very important, although staff will likely try to diminish that importance.

Your goal is to meet and connect with this person, get direct contact information, and open a channel of communication. In many places, that is not only frowned upon but structurally difficult. This is because they do not want you contacting the ED for every little question and complaint. That is not your problem, but it is a legitimate concern on their part. As long as the issue gets resolved, by the ED or by others, who takes care of it is irrelevant. You just want results. But it is always good to know the ED so that your call is always answered.

So how should you encounter the ED for maximum positive responses to issues? First, one must know who the ED is.

The ED is usually, but not always, a woman who either worked in marketing, has a caregiving/nursing background, or both. She or he has moved up the ladder and is there for one reason: financial results. "Nice" people who care about the residents' fun, have huge smiles, love all people, and love to play balloon volleyball are in the activity director's department, not the ED position. EDs make the trains run on time, hire and fire, and get financial results.

That is not to say that great EDs are bad or not nice. I have met many, and most are wonderful people. The nicest and most caring EDs I have met have worked for family-owned communities, not corporate owned. I have also met with and worked with EDs from the corporate culture who left it because they learned that taking great care of residents was not their main job. Maintaining favorable profit margins and complying with corporate controls is how people advance to this critical position. Corporate culture measures profits and losses and has no line item for senior joy or smiles produced.

Marketing people are the wide receivers of the SL world. For non-football-following people, those are the fast guys on the outside on offense who run fast, catch the ball, score touchdowns, and smile at the camera. They tend to be somewhat flashy, get a lot of attention, a lot of money and generally have pretty short careers. In SL reality, they often get a low base salary with incentives based on getting people to move in and pay rent and for services. Generally, the more you pay, the more they get in bonuses, but not always.

The marketing role is often filled by someone who showed talent in another department, like activities. But marketing directors are under huge pressure to perform, so don't be shocked if the person you are working with has been there less than six months. Why? If they perform well in six months, they often get bumped up to another position. If they do not perform well, they are shown the door. Either way, you are dealing with someone with a certain level of pressure and possibly desperation.

Marketing people are not the ones you want to spend a lot of time with despite the fact that most systems are designed to make you do exactly that. Their sole function is to get you to open up your checkbook, move in, and spend the most money possible.

And marketers have zero control over anything once you move in, when things really count. In other words, they can show you slick brochures, hit all the emotional landmines, say the perfect buzzwords, walk the building and show the apartments, and introduce you to key players, *but* if the emergency call system does not work, or there is a leak, or Mom does not like the eggs, a marketer is not going to be of assistance. She, and it almost always is a she, will be unavailable and not the right person to assist. She is busy somewhere else, trying to get the next payday. It is a one-way relationship that often ceases upon move-in, which is when you need her the most.

Which brings us back to the ED. The ED is the one you need to connect with so that when you call on that rare and important occasion, your call is answered. Remember that in the average community of, let's say, 130 units, there are approximately 120 live-in residents, 50 to 60 staff members, random family members, numerous home health nurses, occasional state licensing visitors, people calling out of their shifts last second, outside vendors, activity entertainers, and marketers all seeking the ED's attention "just for a second." So if you do not luck out and get the ED on the phone, it is not personal. But if you are a nervous Nellie, call daily, or are hard to deal with, you may not get a call back.

How do you navigate this gauntlet of smiling people so that you can best take care of your loved one? Remember, you want to speak with the ED. You will likely have to meet the marketing person as well, but meeting with the ED is key. You may have to schedule an appointment, but that is fine. Once you meet with them, there are three ways to stand out positively.

1. **Show you know what you are talking about.** You do not have to be an RN or LVN to have an intelligent and refined conversation, which is the goal and will set you apart. You need only know what is in this book to be the hero. By asking the right questions, dropping Title 22 into the conversation at the right moment, making eye contact, and taking notes, you will distinguish yourself from 90 percent of the other tours and families.

2. **Research the ED.** Get the ED's name and use Google to find out his or her background. Find a common interest. When people share personal information with each other, they

connect, so when you call, the ED will have a positive feeling about you and your family member.

3. **Know about the industry.** This is the big one. There are questions to show you are educated and intelligent, and then there are simple information-gathering questions. The questions to show you are educated focus on the mechanics of the operations, the regulations of Title 22 of the Health and Safety Code of the State of California, and the fees. I included a set of questions that deal with these topics in chapter 12.

The ED is the one who can get on the phone or the walkie-talkie and move mountains. The ED controls the building and staff and is the fastest road to happiness. A great ED is a blessing, and you will know if that person is a good person and has a big heart by how residents are dealt with. One secret goal you have is to see or hear an real interaction between a resident and the ED. I am not saying you should snoop. I am saying if you happen notice an interaction, perhaps hang around and listen and then go to the resident after the ED leaves and ask if he or she is always that nice. Older people tend to have little to no filter and tend to not care whom they offend, so they will likely tell you the truth. But this is just a precursor to your meeting with the most important person in the entire building, the chef.

Chapter 12
THE HIT LIST

The Hit List is the key questions you need to ask the staff. The questions and topics vary in importance, but each contains a key issue that you may not think is important at the moment, but that will become very important down the line when it may to be too late to pivot. **Understand the landscape now and save yourself and your family heartache later**.

1. LEVELS OF CARE

In chapter 7, we discussed the ABCs of senior living, so you now understand the basics of the system. The time, however, has come to go deeper. There are two entry points into SL. People either come in when they are younger and relatively healthy, or they come in older and in need of AL and a significant amount of care. In the late 1990s, when I began, it was mostly the former who became our clients—older but healthy people who had become isolated and no longer wished to endure the grind of living as a single person alone, unsafe, and often bored. These independent people thrived in senior living, as they were now surrounded by other seniors and no longer isolated, and looked forward to activities and meals. They also enjoyed not having to do the cooking and cleaning and other menial tasks.

They would naturally age and, at some point, need assistance with daily tasks. The family or the community would notice that the resident was not taking his or her meds properly or had fallen in the shower due to balance issues, and then the individual would join the AL side of the program, in which they paid a monthly fee for medication management and possibly other services. And so enters the twist that most people do not expect, even though it is completely predictable. The community will not stress this issue although they hope it will occur. People are worried about declining abilities and increasing costs, so neither side brings it up. That is an error that can hurt you.

Why? Because you need to know what you are looking at financially and otherwise. **Most people fail to properly budget.** They focus only on rent, which is wrong on multiple levels. First of all, most places annually increase rent by 3 to 6 percent. Everything in your life goes up annually, so it makes sense that the rent does too. But as Father Time continues his march, people's abilities decline. Fact of life. To understand what things will cost if your loved one is lucky enough to live deep into their eighties, nineties, or even their hundreds, you need to be prepared.

Most communities separate the people who are independent from those who have care. Full stop. Think about that. The community does this to make operations more efficient and to cut response time and labor costs. They may have different floors, or wings, or even different buildings. Ask that question and listen carefully to the answer. This is something people often hear but do not absorb, because what this means is that when Mom or Dad needs care, they have to move out of the comfy apartment that has become their home and into a different apartment in a different location. This is *very* disruptive to the resident, who has become familiar with the space and is finally at home in it. They know their neighbors and have memorized the path to the dining room and other locations. Do not discount the importance of that. Their comfort is taken away by the move at a time when they need that comfort and familiarity the most. Seniors hate and fear change.

The first key question, if Mom is currently independent, is what happens when care or services are required? Will they move her? To where? You should ask to see that place and see if it is where you want Mom to end up because, if she remains healthy and ages in place well, at some point that is where she is likely to live. No one will tell you that. The reason no one will tell you that is those areas are sometimes not as spiffy or nice as the ones in the glossy brochures. Or they are smaller and often significantly more expensive. In most cases, the moving of people and separation is not because it is better for your parent. It can, in fact, have negative psychological consequences for the senior. You need to know the probable future here and do your homework now because surprise is not what you want to experience. I am telling you this because nearly every resident and family exhibits resistance to this evolution even when it is obvious and necessary. People resist because of change, they resist because of increased costs and the overall hassle of having to move again.

At Sunnycrest, I did not separate the independent from those receiving care. My philosophy was that by not separating those who needed extra services, we kept them feeling normal and made as little change as possible to keep their issues private and their confidence level high. Yes, it would have been more efficient to put them on a different wing or floor, but I would not want my family moved around for the convenience of the operator, so I chose not to do that to my clients.

But if the building and operations you like do separate, tour it now. Determine if it is acceptable before you get that call or letter explaining that the staff sees a decline in Mom or sudden "unusual behavior." It starts with a suggestion that you take her to the doctor and have them examine her and review her meds, but by then you should realize what is to come. She is going to need care, and 95 percent of the time, they are right. She should be where she is safest, and many wellness directors or care coordinators understand that their job is to keep residents safe and take care of them first and foremost. But don't be naïve. They know that income from AL services is good for business. And the people who have the highest amount of care, and thus paying the highest fees, are also most likely to be leaving the community for an even higher level of care, taking that income with them.

Some people or places see AL as the ticket to fat profits and will "nudge" a family into AL. It will be under the label of doing what is best for Mom, of course, but they also have an ulterior financial motive. The people I worked with put the residents and their best interests first, and while people would resist when we told them they or their family member needed care, they understood and accepted it because we had built up such goodwill and credibility. You want that kind of place.

So, in summary, ask for and check out the AL charges and see where and how those people are living. That is your future. If you're lucky.

TIP: AL fees are sometimes negotiable, especially if you have more than one service. No one will tell you this, but it is often true. For example, the most common service is medication management, in which the community orders the meds, hands them out at the right time and place to the resident, and reorders when needed. That generally costs $300/month, which is quite a bargain when you realize that is about $10/day, and he/she is getting meds likely three times a day, so $3 per visit is low. Now places have gotten smarter and do it by volume of pills or number of visits. The second most common service is ambulating. Ambulating is getting a wheelchair and giving the resident a ride to and from the dining room or to and from activities. The fees can range for a variety of reasons, but let us just say that it is $200/month. If Mom is paying only for rent and now needs both, you are looking at an additional $500/month fee on top of the rent. Know that they do not love to negotiate, but many places do. Suggesting, for example, a $400 compromise for both will not be met with smiles, but may be met with a yes. It only results in a savings of $1,200/year, but that is your $1,200. Bank it for later just in case.

2. RENT INCREASES

Everyone who rents an apartment knows that rent increases come annually. Senior living is no different. However, to my knowledge, unlike rent-control apartment buildings, there are no restrictions on rent increases in private-pay senior living. The bad news is they can do whatever they want. The good news is that, by law, they are required to have a rate disclosure statement available to you. In California, this is the California Rate Disclosure statement pursuant to the California Health and Safety Code Section 1569.658. It is required and intended to provide you with a listing of increases in the average monthly rent as well as the average percentage of the increase. The last three years of rent increases, if any, should be listed, but fees for optional services were not legally required last time I checked. This document is supposed to be given to all prospective residents of the community *before* payment of any part of the community fee or execution of a residency agreement.

Rent increases vary between 3 and 6 percent. I usually did 5 percent. That barely kept up with the cost of living and salaries, but some communities raise the rent much more. You should know this now and factor it in.

3. LICENSING REPORTS

Ask about the community's relationship and history with state licensing. That question will likely be answered with a smile no matter what. You will also likely be the first person to ever ask. In years of doing tours, no one ever asked me, but I was always ready for it. The good news is that you will know in advance if their answer is true thanks to reading this book.

State licensing is a book unto itself, but I will try to make this quick and painless. Other than some basic guidelines about the hot water temperature range and simple and logical rules of how to lead, the rule book is like the baseball rule book. It is up to the umpire on the field.

State licensing regulators, known as LPAs, are a different breed. They are well-meaning people with a lot of power and wide-ranging life experiences. If they wanted to, they could give nearly every building a failing score by digging through the garbage. Or they could give nearly every building a perfect score. Two LPAs could see the same thing and have completely different responses. Some LPAs are magnificent and smart and worldly and are people to be respected and even admired. Some I dealt with were wise, smart, and knowledgeable. Others, not so much. With some, you wonder if they have any life experience at all, especially the newer ones, who tend to want to show they are in charge and expect you to bow down even if they know nothing.

You might have picked up on this, but I am not bowing down to anyone. So it is safe to say that I had my issues with state licensing, especially early on in my career. Coming from the daily, barroom-brawling criminal court and into SL where I was judged by someone with a flawed system of investigation, did not work for me. I fought and argued and paid the price. Why? Because the regulators are like the government. They never admit they are wrong, and a few wield power like they came down from Mt. Olympus. Plus, once they put something in writing, it is there forever. And if you disagree with your LPA, who is the arbitrator of impartiality judging and deciding whether the state licensing official was right or wrong? Well, that would be another state licensing official.

I appealed something years ago, lost with a rubber stamp ruling, and appealed it to the higher-up. I think I am still waiting for a ruling, and I have been out of the business for nearly a year. Bottom line is if I was wrong or my employees did something wrong, then we man up, fix it, and do better next time. But if it was a bad call, I was ready for war. Just because I left the public defender's office did not mean that the public defender in me left as well.

Licensing, overall, does an amazing job. They have a nearly impossible task, not nearly enough staff, and arcane rules. They must, for example, follow up on certain matters in a certain period of time. This makes them a yo-yo to the whims of the elderly. Remove the blinders and understand that just because you become old does not mean you suddenly transform into an angel. I have seen older people lie and cheat and manipulate more, and more effectively, than anyone else in my life. And that is saying something for someone who spent years defending alleged criminals.

Check out the communities you are looking at to understand their relationship with state licensing. This will tell you about visits by the state, citations, inspections, complaints, and other reports. You are looking for a record of problems and if there are systemic problems. Everyone has inspections and complaints. That is not unusual. Your focus should be on the annual inspections and if the allegations are substantiated, inconclusive, or unfounded. The allegations, if substantiated, can result in a Type A or Type B citation. Type A can mean an immediate health-safety or personal-rights issue of a serious nature. Type B is less serious, and while an A seems frightening, it may not be what your imagination comes up with. *Substantiated* means the complaint was determined to be valid or true; *inconclusive* means they could not say yes or no; and *unfounded* is the rarest of all birds, a lie. In other words, it was false, could not have happened, or is totally unreasonable. Sadly, this happens more than you would guess.

The big picture is that licensing is there to protect the weak and aged. That is a valid and important job that we all agree must be maintained and that mandate fulfilled. Even the best places have an occasional allegation that leads to a substantiated allegation, and when you have hundreds of residents and dozens of staff and people everywhere, mistakes will be made. The good news is that you do not have to go to the licensing offices to pull the documents. You can go online to the Department of Social Services website (www.cdss.ca.gov) and search for a community by name or facility number, which is on all cards and marketing material. When you find it, go to "facility detail" and read the visits and complaints. Issues regarding food should be looked into, as well as abuse of any kind. While those two are rare and you may find a lot of information that seems not too terrible, it is better to know everything now. The community is required to post these in a visible location.

4. LONGEVITY AND LEADERSHIP

The better the company and operations, the greater the longevity of its employees. I say this for two reasons. One is that, when I was an employee, I learned that organizations that do not value their people do not retain the best talent. The people who stay are not the stars; many average people rise to the top simply out of attrition. But your goal should be to join the best and most stable organization. Most people never consider that they are joining a team or "buying the company stock" by signing up and moving in.

At my community, I valued my employees and created an employee-centric system. I focused daily on residents and their families but also on keeping employees happy and their morale high. This is no easy task; it made us stand out in the industry, and my scoreboard defined success as longevity of key staff. My goal was to find great talent and retain them by keeping them happy. The perfect prospective employee was someone who had been professionally screwed over. That was one of my many secrets in the hiring process, because those people tended to appreciate a great owner and especially one with some depth. While another employer could always pay more, my approach was to nurture and empower great staff so that, if they were smart enough, they would turn into long-term employees. My loyalty would be matched (hopefully) by their loyalty, and the big winner would be my residents. At the time I left the business, my ED had been with me almost six years, my maintenance supervisor over twelve, and my chef close to sixteen years.

Therefore, the suggestion here is to check how long the key players have been with this company and, most importantly, in this specific location. It does not help you if they have been with the company ten years if they stay at this location for only one. The best scenario is that you and your family are dealing with the same people and having long-term reliable relationships. Most places shuffle people in and out, requiring constant reboots and starting from scratch, which hurts you. This is important because it is disconcerting to meet and establish a relationship and communication pipeline with someone who is not going to be there tomorrow. You seek longevity and stability. Ask the ED and all the key players you meet how long they have been in this location and with this company, and whether they have plans to leave. Knowing whom you are dealing with is important for long-term success.

5. THE FOOD EFFECT

Food is the hottest issue in most SL communities. Why? Because three times a day residents get to rate, discuss, and criticize something. The women, who make up the majority of the population and who cooked a million meals for their families and friends, love to pick apart the food and explain how it is not as good as they would make.

My community served three meals daily in the dining room 365 days a year. That meant that I would be graded by nearly every resident multiple times, as meals are the big social events of almost every day. Nearly everyone feels that their input on the meal is not only something you should know but a birthright. I get it and never shied away from it. In fact, I welcomed it.

Be sure to ask if you can have a meal in the dining room at the same time the residents are eating. You want to observe the service and presentation, try the food, and most importantly, see how the staff relates to residents in action. Do not tell them in advance that you want to do this, or they will stage a perfect meal—you want to see the real deal.

Let your mouth vote as to how the food is, but let your eyes and ears wander and see the vibe of the dining room. If you want a predictor of a successful life at this community, start with dining-room dynamics, and food in particular is ground zero.

6. WALK IT AGAIN BUT WITHOUT THEM SHADOWING YOU

When you are leaving, your final (exit) question is not really a question but a statement. Say that you intend to come back unannounced, possibly with another family member, and just want their approval. They will tell you that you need to call and make arrangements so they can shadow you. Nicely ask them if Mom moves, in, do they need to call in advance when they plan to visit? The answer will naturally be no, and that is the perfect moment to share that you are seriously considering this location but want to feel like it is a friendly place where family is always welcome. Their response should be that you are welcome anytime but just to check in with the front desk, as they need to know who is in the building. That is the correct answer. Smile, tell them that their community is in the top three, and leave. That is just enough to whet their appetites but not enough to make them feel they have you in the bag. You are setting them up for the next call or meeting.

In summary, the goal of **The Hit List** is to provide you the key questions that you need to ask and the secret moves that give you and your family the knowledge to make an informed decision. The questions and topics contained here are those that can bring happiness, or could easily T-bone you once Mom moves in, as they are matters you likely cannot control or change. This can potentially save you and your loved one's heartache, and can increase the likelihood of success. By following these simple steps, you are far and away not only the most knowledgeable potential customer they have likely seen, but you are well on your way to acquiring all the key information critical to making the right decision, putting your family member in a position to be successful short- and long-term, and earning that hero medal.

Chapter 13
THE HIDDEN CHAPTER

This chapter is hidden. It contains never-before-shared vignettes and a secret trick to save you money. In order to uncover it, you must go to my website, www.unicornseniorliving.com, and find the icon of a little treasure chest. To unlock the secrets and the stories, first answer the inquiry as to which three chapters in this book are your favorites in order of which you liked the most, and then click the treasure icon and enter the code word **BONUS** to get a special hidden treat.

Enjoy.

David

Chapter 14
THE REAL MOST IMPORTANT PERSON AND THE GRAVY

As previously mentioned, the most important daily issue in most SL communities is food. In real estate it is *location, location, location,* but in senior living it is *food, food, food.*

Three times a day, residents put on their judge's hats, rate and discuss (and criticize) something, and do so as an absolute authority. This is a big thing for people who are no longer asked their opinions about work matters, or of the world in general. They relish the opportunity to be an authority, and they know food and what they enjoy just like you and I do. How often do you go to a restaurant and discuss how much or how little you liked the food and/or service? Every time! Seniors are no different.

Women, who make up the majority of the senior population, and who cooked a million meals for their family and friends, may love to pick apart your food when you cook for them in your home, so imagine how they are regarding food cooked by a stranger they are paying, especially when they know no one can ever bark back at them. The staff is trained to take it no matter what is said to them and to always be polite and respectful to the residents. Residents might simply compliment the food (which happens a lot), or they will criticize it and say it is not as good as they would make. If the meal is not pleasurable, it is a stark reminder that they are not in control of something as basic as what foods they are consuming. Meals are a key part of life in senior living and why the most important person in the building is the chef.

The ED is the brains of the building. But the backbone of every community is the chef. He or she can make the community shine or sputter. The reason is simple. Proper nutrition is critical for seniors, the lack of which is the cause of many of their problems. If the residents like and eat the food and the menu is balanced and intelligent, their nutritional needs will be met and they will be physically stronger and mentally sharper. Nutrition and overmedication are (in my nonmedical opinion) the biggest variables surrounding the joy and safety of seniors. How often do seniors stop eating regularly and then appear depressed? Not eating properly can have a negative impact on the efficacy of their medicines. Medications are often intended and designed to be taken with food. Take away proper and balanced food, and you have an unstable, depressed, or ill senior. Good food is critical.

Now let us step back and see the big picture. My community served three meals daily in the dining room 365 days a year. That is approximately 1,100 meals a year per person, and with 125 people in-house, that is 137,500 opportunities to either enjoy or complain about a meal. Seniors may not be consumed with "liking" things on Facebook or giving reviews and taking pictures of every meal like on Yelp, but that does not mean they do not have opinions they want known and shared.

From my position as ED, each complaint can drive you crazy and derail whatever issue or project you are working on—a distraction at best or a crisis at worst. You never know if the complaint is isolated or part of a greater issue that needs serious investigation, so as the ED, you are always on high alert with food.

I used to sit with residents and eat the same food that they were. My presence encouraged complaints because residents (like parents) want to keep you humble and feeling like your potential is greater than you are delivering. Residents often view staff as their "children" who need guidance and input. They have a vested interest in improving everything, and telling you things are bad forces attention on any issue. Conversely, most figure that saying everything is perfect will not help them even if it is true. There are outliers, and people who are just honest and not so Machiavellian, but for most, they are working you. Let your own taste buds tell you the truth.

That is what I did. I would sit with the residents at a table in the dining room and eat the same food they were eating. They *loved* that, because who doesn't like to meet the boss and have an opportunity to go one-on-one? I did this as often as possible because it caused several things to occur. One, everyone saw me and recognized me and loved that I was doing it. The message was that I cared and was clearly testing the kitchen and their performance. It also said, on the macro level, that everyone was accountable. The chef would also know I was checking up on him, and he never knew when I would show up.

If I did not like the meal, I believed that the residents would not like it. I would then privately sit with the chef and give my honest feedback. If I liked it, I took any complaints with a grain of salt, if they existed at all. Nothing was better than the joy I would have sharing a delicious and nutritious meal with the residents and hearing about how they loved the meal, or the latest activity or hire or whatever. By not hiding and being somewhat available and vulnerable, I bred a level of respect both ways.

But that is not to say people were always honorable or honest about it.

Let me take a moment and share with you one of the seminal moments of my ED career. It was Thanksgiving, probably around 1999 or 2000, and I had decided to spend it with the residents and staff. We were struggling to turn things around back then, and my being there sent a message to residents and staff (and their families) as to how important I thought they were.

It was a classic Thanksgiving meal: turkey with mashed potatoes and gravy. I ate with some of the residents who had no family. After we were done, I walked around the dining room wishing everyone a Happy Thanksgiving, talking about what we were grateful for, and putting smiles on everyone's faces. I also performed my secret test of any meal: the clean plate test. If the meal was a success, the plates would be clean.

Looking around the space, I could see that nearly all the plates were clean. They had eaten everything and loved it. The food was excellent, so I understood why. Person after person was happy and complimentary. I went table to table to see if anyone wanted seconds.

Until I got to Pauline (not her real name). Pauline was a mean and harsh person. She was only happy being unhappy. A true Dragon Senior.

As I got to her table, the smile ran away from my face, but I plastered it back on as best I could, wished her a Happy Thanksgiving, and asked if she wanted seconds.

"This food is crap!" she yelled at the top of her lungs. The entire dining room, which had been full of buzz, went silent. "The turkey is dry, and the gravy tastes like it came out of a can. The chef is horrible, and I would not serve this food to a dog!" My heart stopped.

A swirl of responses and reactions flew through my mind. I looked around to realize every eye in the room was focused on me and on what my reaction would be. I was in an impossible dilemma.

"I ate the exact same food as you, and, frankly, I thought it was great, and looking around the room and having spoken to almost everyone here, they all agree with me. The food is good; I know it."

"The food was horrible, especially the gravy, and there was not nearly enough of it." She was glaring me down, and no one in the room was breathing.

"Well, if the food, and specifically the gravy, was so terrible," I asked, "why in the world would you want more of it?" My logic caught her off guard. She froze.

"That's Pauline for you!" some voice in the back said, and suddenly the entire dining room erupted in laughter. "She hates the gravy and wants more of it!" Everyone cracked up with the absurdity of her latest attack, and the tense moment evaporated.

I leaned over and whispered to her that I would like to speak to her privately when she was finished with her meal.

I called her family to discuss what had happened and why I was upset. Her son called her a word I will not use here, said that she was a terrible person, and said they did not want her toxicity around them anymore.

She finally walked into my office and closed the door. She sat down, and I said one word. "Why?"

"Why what?" she replied.

"Why did you lie and try so hard to embarrass and humiliate me?" I asked.

She was looking down at her shoes now and did not reply.

"Why?" I repeated, wanting to know before I decided what to do.

"You want to know why?" she replied. "Because my son hates me, and his family hates me, and they never come to visit, and they never call, and it's Thanksgiving, and I should be with them. And he won't take my calls, and I can't speak with him, and you kind of look like him, and I can't yell at him, so I yelled at you because he's around your age and you kind of remind me of him." And, with that, the dam burst, and she began crying hysterically.

"So this was not about the gravy?"

"No, this had nothing to do with the stupid gravy; the gravy was great," she said through the tears and tissues.

After the holidays, I asked her if she might be happier at a different community. She thought it also might be time for a fresh start.

Sometimes, it's not about the food. Many residents have peripheral issues that they cannot conquer or heal for a variety of reasons, so they lash out at the easiest targets: the staff, and the chef in particular, or the food. She was a very rare, nasty person, and she is the perfect example of why some people fear senior living. She was the one person who was with us because her family could not stand her. The other 124 were wonderful people, but TV and movies would make you believe she is, at a minimum, reflective of the type of person that lives in senior living. That would be a total falsehood. But I shared this story anyway because it serves multiple purposes, and now you know why complaints about food do not always trigger Kennedy assassination–level investigations.

But sometimes it is, which is why having an amazing chef is critical. The chef is not only responsible for keeping the residents healthy and happy, but also keeping your food costs manageable. What you do not want, as my beloved former chef used to say, is the most expensive trash cans in the city: cans full of expensive food that residents do not like. Controlling costs and serving a good product on time is a balancing act for sure, and as an operator, no one can hurt the operations as much as a lousy chef.

In addition, you need someone you can talk to about special diets and who will listen to praise and criticism equally, and who can bring out the human side with a resident when no one else can. The chef is uniquely able, in my experience, to reach people otherwise unreachable through the common experience of favorite foods. He or she needs to be able to reach a resident who may be down or declining, and find out what they love to eat (and make it for them), where they are from, and possibly just give them a little TLC. It may not be in the formal job description, but any competent chef needs to have that something extra in order to see happy and full residents. This secret sauce can be critical in turning around someone who is down and seemingly out, and bringing them back. I've seen it dozens of times. Build up the nutrition, get them eating healthy and consistently again, and watch them rebloom. That is what a great chef can do.

For the average situation, meeting the chef and discussing your favorite foods, any special diets, favorite dishes, and unusual culinary desires may not bring perfection, but it will clue the chef into what your situation is and give you a beachhead for later success. If they are not enjoying the food, and you had spoken to the chef early on, now is a perfect time to reconnect and discuss what can be done to improve the intake and happiness level. But having that conversation during the dating period is much better than after you are married because, if you get the cold shoulder or they indicate no interest in your family member, I would be very concerned and not optimistic about long-term success.

In conclusion, you want to meet and get to know the chef before you commit. The chef is the heart of the entire operation. Try to get a sense of their routine schedule so you know when they are in-house in case you ever want to chat. You may only come on the weekends, and you want to be able to say hi and share a word when needed. And I would also have at least two meals (a lunch and a dinner or a breakfast and a dinner) to get a sense of the program and the vibe of the dining room. Food is the key to remaining healthy and balanced, so take this relationship seriously, and know that a great chef can be your best friend and greatest ally.

Chapter 15
CRIMINAL LAW FOR DUMMIES

With such a heavy subject as the future of your parents' lives, perhaps a brief break from the emotionally exhausting subject is in order. Writing this book has opened up my mental floodgates as to the past. This experience has been wonderful on so many levels, including my many years in SL.

I once inhabited a world with zero connection to senior living. That subject was the last thing I thought about, and my life consisted of criminal law only. I ate, breathed, and dreamed criminal law. Like many things in my life, I had never intended to get involved in it at all. In fact, I thought of it as a nasty, dirty, and scary world to be avoided.

Near the end of the first year of law school, students are interviewed for summer jobs. This is a significant time in which grades are suddenly crucial, and a pecking order of talent is established based on which firms hire which students. Generally, the students with the best grades get the best internships at the best firms. In 1987, I had worked on Capitol Hill as a legislative intern and, in the summer of 1988, was very much looking forward to finally getting out of the classroom and library and into the real world.

Students receive a list of firms that will be coming to interview. The students request interviews, and the firms review the list. A schedule is produced of who is being interviewed and when. In one room, three serious-looking people sat waiting for me. I had just completed my interview with the civil firm I was most likely to work for, and the interview had gone well. The pressure was off. I arrived at this one, and one interviewer immediately got in my face. Taken aback, I asked to be reminded which firm they represented.

"The Los Angeles County Office of the Public Defender." I had not applied to interview with them, so I politely stated that a mistake had been made, got up and thanked them for their time.

"Professor Broderick contacted us about you. He wants you interviewed. He says you should work for us," said the man who had aggressively started in on me initially. I was confused. Broderick was a former prosecutor and former US attorney. Why had a prosecutor recommended me for a criminal defense job?

"Sit down," the lady said. "We are not going to bite." She was a beauty, so I sat.

They peppered me with bizarre questions, scenarios, and hypotheticals. It was kind of a fascinating interview, and I probably would have been nervous except it was meaningless as I had secured a job, and these people were never going to hire me. The person who had walked out of the room as I walked in was on law review, and let's just say I was not on law review and leave it at that.

At the end, we shook hands, and I went to see Broderick and asked him if he had suggested me and why. He said that, as a prosecutor, the system only works properly if the defense attorneys are great, sharp, and fierce. That if the side representing the defendants is passive or fearful, the prosecution, with the cops and the courts on their side, creates an imbalance, and justice is not achieved. He told me that few have the talent, passion, and backbone to be a defense attorney, to stand up to the abuse and fight and still have moral clarity. He said I was going to be a defense attorney and a great one at that.

I thought he was insane. With a smile, I thanked him and walked away.

Weeks later, the firm I was going to be working for sent me a letter that, due to the bad economy, they were not hiring as many interns, and I was out. Describing how devastated I was is not possible. Everything hinged on that summer job, and suddenly I was out.

The next day I received a letter. The public defender's office offered me the job.

What followed was ten years of insanity, hilarity, sadness, tears, blood, and guts. I learned more about life, and about myself, in my time in the PD's office than at any other point of my life. I am tremendously grateful to them for affording me this incredible opportunity. It was real life but with the dial turned up to eleven.

Allow me to share some of the funny stuff that you simply will not believe. I will start with some of my least favorite stories that you will find surprising.

In the PD's office, you work in many courthouses, and they move you around so you do not get too comfortable with one place. The good side is that you have anonymity and more privacy.

One day, I was in my local supermarket. I liked to shop late when it was empty after a long day at work. As I was checking out, the cashier says, "Oh my God!"

I looked around to see who he was looking at only to discover he was looking at me. "You saved my life!" he said, grabbing my hand and shaking it like he had just met the president. He explained that I had represented him in court a year before. He had gotten into trouble, and I had gotten his sentence knocked down to disturbing the peace, with a small fine. He had learned from it and turned his life around, and it was all because of me. I had no idea who this guy was or why he would not let go of my hand. I represented twenty to thirty people a day every day for years and had no idea who he was but was happy to have helped him.

As I walked away, I turned, looked around and saw that no one else in the market was close or listening, and asked him what he had originally been charged with. "Masturbating in public," he said with a huge smile. I thought of our handshake. I never went back to that market again.

I call this chapter "Criminal Law for Dummies" because, initially, it was suggested that I contact the "Dummies" series publisher and see if they wanted to produce the book, *Senior Living for Dummies*. But I do not like the "for dummies" part, and I did not want to be part of someone else's thing because I wanted to keep this 100 percent me.

At the beginning of one's career in criminal law, you do a lot of low-level stuff until you really know what you are doing. You learn on the job, and random cases come to you. You do the very best you can under the limitations.

One day, when I was working in the Van Nuys courthouse, I was handed a case of possession and prostitution. The young lady, named Julie, was a confused-looking simpleton. The police report stated that she had been walking the streets and got picked up by a john; they bought some crack to smoke, and as they drove to have their little party, they got pulled over. She then got arrested while already being on probation for a similar offense.

When two or more people are arrested at the same time, step one is to make sure the office did not represent the second defendant simultaneously, because they may have different and conflicting interests and defenses. It appeared, however, that I could not determine the identity of the second person.

Something about the case bugged me. I was very new and had little idea what I was doing, but my instincts said something was wrong with this story. The missing identity of the second person was odd, and Julie was going to jail no matter what due to the previous conviction and the probation violation. She was cooked.

This is where PDs earn their paycheck. Making lemonade out of lemons or, in this case, out of crack. We have terrible cases, and clients who do such stupid things are beyond comprehension. We save them daily.

Having nothing to work with, I called my investigator. All I had was a license plate number. She was the passenger, so there must have been a driver. I gave the weird license number, which was something like DACHEF, and asked him to run it. Thirty minutes later he called me up and said, "Do you know what you have just done? The license plate belongs to the chief of the fire department. Your hooker got picked up by him. They apparently went to score some crack and got arrested. They were covering it up, and you figured it out. The press might be coming. You're about to be hit by a huge s#*& storm."

DACHEF meant "The Chief." The cops had arrested both of them and then scrubbed the police report, maybe as a professional courtesy, and that is why I could not find the codefendant. I had stepped on a landmine, but now that it was out, they would have to prosecute him, and that meant they would need her to testify against him. Suddenly, I had leverage.

I went to the prosecutor, whose face was now redder than a baboon's behind, and told him that he was going to dismiss the case against her and put her in drug rehab instead of jail for the probation violation so she could get some help. In exchange, she would testify against DACHEF. I had him and he knew it.

We agreed to delay the case until the smoke cleared so that we could work out the deal. The press jumped all over me, and I said a few things to them, and it was over. The next day, however, in the Metro section of the *Los Angeles Times*, there was a huge article with a picture of me and her on the front page. By the time I got to work, everyone (except for me) had seen it, and I was the target of admiration, jealousy, and mockery from my colleagues. People joked that I had the "magic touch" and was suddenly the "golden boy." PDs rarely get attention that private counsel do, so I was a mini-celebrity for a good five minutes. In the end, my boss told me he was taking the case away because the senior attorneys complained that the "newbie" should not keep it. I was later told that the deal I had set up did not happen, and I was upset about it for months and never forgave my boss.

Los Angeles County's population is bigger than fifteen of the nation's states. It is enormous. If LA County were a state, it would be the eighth largest in the union, with ten million people. That is a lot of people and a lot of cases. I once tried to figure out how many people I represented during my time with the PD's office. I stopped counting when I got above five thousand.

One of the funny highlights (or lowlights, depending on how you wish to look at it) of my career was a prostitution case in Hollywood (I worked in Hollywood a long time and was actually sworn in by Judge Wapner, the son of the legendary Judge Joe Wapner of TV fame). Another prostitution case, another sad story.

This young lady apparently worked in the sketchiest massage parlor in Hollywood, which was really saying something. Long story short, the vice squad arrested her for soliciting an officer. Pretty basic stuff until I interviewed her. She stated that the man told her he was a cop and had gotten a special massage in exchange for leaving her and the others alone, and then had turned around and arrested her anyway. I had heard girls say this many times before.

She was prepared to go to jail. I asked her if she could describe anything unusual or specific about him physically that only someone who had seen him without clothes would know. Officers are not allowed to engage in illegal activity, obviously, so if he was naked and she could prove it, then I had something.

"No," she said sadly, "but he did leave his socks. I kept them." They did not give her time to get her shoes, so she had grabbed them in the chaos of the arrest and put them on for warmth.

"Where are those socks now?" I asked. She pulled them out of her purse. They were basic black socks, but they had an odd small insignia that made them distinct. That was all I needed.

I went to the prosecutor, pulled him aside, and told him he should dismiss the case. We had worked together for quite a while and trusted each other to a point.

In front of the officer, I told the prosecutor that I had something that would prove the officer was lying about what happened, and that they needed to dismiss the case. The prosecutor wanted specifics, but I could not reveal my hand in case I got stonewalled and had to play my only card during trial. The officer, however, was a big and very intimidating guy, and he was eyeballing me hard. When the prosecutor told me to pound sand and walked away, I suggested to the cop that he get the prosecutor to dismiss. He was rattled by my confidence and stared as I walked across the now empty courtroom. When I got to the other side, I looked around, and with no one else watching, I pulled his sock out of my pocket. At first it did not register, but when I put my finger on the insignia, the smile ran away from his face and he looked queasy. I raised my eyebrows while staring at him, and he left the room.

Minutes later the prosecutor came back in and told me that the officer had been called away for an emergency so they wanted a continuance. I told him what he could do with his request. They dismissed the case later that day.

My client was stunned and propositioned me on the spot (in front of the prosecutor). I declined and thanked her and suggested she seek a different profession. She declined and, within a month, was rearrested and went to jail.

After all of this silliness, the prosecutor asked me what I had up my sleeve. We had built up a respect for one another, and we went into a side room where I explained it all and showed him the socks. They asked if they could have them. I declined until I spoke to my supervisor. My supervisor felt that they would best handle it internally, so he told me to give him the socks, which I did. I never saw that cop again.

Have you been sufficiently distracted from old people and senior living? If yes, then I have rebooted you and we can get back on topic here. It is too bad, because I was just about to tell you how I represented Ice Cube (before he was famous) and what happened when he was asked to sing. I guess that will have to wait for the sequel to this book.

Chapter 16
SMART PREPPING FOR THE MOVE

With this little breather behind us, it is time to get to the nuts and bolts of the move and the critical importance of making a pre-move-in checklist. Time and time again, this part of the equation seems to catch everyone off guard. Lack of planning and preparation of the conceptual, legal, and economic sides of the equation is often a source of unnecessary pain and stress. Don't be that person. Many of these elements you can and should start right now.

1. **Documents.** It is shocking how many elderly people do not have wills, advance health-care directives for medical decisions, durable power-of-attorney documents, medical information release forms, and DNRs. These are things that younger people must have as well, but for seniors, there is no excuse. Your express wishes *must* be codified in writing, or what you want to occur may not. This can and likely will lead to consequences that could horrify you, so please find someone you trust and take care of these matters. It will be time and money well spent and will give you peace

of mind that your wishes will be fulfilled. Do not wait to address these matters.

2. **Downsizing.** Let's call it "rightsizing" instead. The reality is that seniors accumulate a lot of stuff they don't need, do not know they have, and do not use. Go through a closet, drawer, or room and ask your mom and dad the last time they looked at its contents. Ninety percent of the time, they did not even know what was inside. Start this rightsizing process now. Not only will you be able to reduce what you will need to pay to move, but you will have a chance to hear stories and choose things that remind everyone of special times. However long you think this rightsizing will take, multiply it by ten.

3. **eBay.** Much of what you will find will be completely unnecessary for the senior or you. Much will be trash, but some will be valuable. With the senior's permission, engage one of the younger family members to put this stuff on eBay or Craigslist to lighten the load and

make some money. You may be shocked at how valuable some of their stuff is, and they may enjoy the possibility of not only making some money but also having something they feel attached to in their new home. Maybe have the younger person do research and advise Nana what has market value, so that expectations are realistic. But keep eyes wide open. Just because Nana does not realize the value of her newspaper from the day after JFK was assassinated does not mean that a collector will not. Often seniors may not even realize what treasures they have, and all too often after someone passes, family cannot deal and just bring in people to trash everything. You would be amazed what treasures can be found.

4. **Photos.** This is the time to not only collect the photos, but to digitize and review them with him or her. Put names to the faces. Understand the roots and hear the stories. I recommend videotaping these discussions. In ten years, when your child wants to know the family history and you are a little fuzzy as to their heritage, you will be glad you did. The process may also bring everyone closer and help the

senior realize the importance of transferring this information.

5. **Money.** This is a touchy subject but one you must engage. All too often, seniors have lost control and understanding of their finances. Many are hyperfocused on this subject, but others sometimes forget budgets or spending limits, or about accounts entirely. In addition, seniors now appear to be the number-one target of fraud. They are perceived as lonely, vulnerable, and easily ripped off, with little energy to go after the perpetrators or too much shame to admit they have been swindled. Financial abuse of the elderly is not only on the rise; it has reached epidemic proportions, and most keep it a secret, even from their families. Credit-card applications are generally not shredded by seniors and are stolen from abandoned trash cans. With the seniors' permission, check out their finances and stop anything fishy before it is too late. Also, check out government websites that list unclaimed money. So far, everyone to whom I have suggested checking out state and federal

websites has found money owed to them. That
will put a smile on their faces.

6. **Veterans benefits.** It is shocking how many
seniors (and their families) do not know that
veterans are entitled to money for senior living
under certain government rules. These monies
help pay for AL and can take some of the
pressure off the financial side of this decision.
There is much political debate currently as to
the way the country often fails to properly take
care of its veterans, especially with all of the
talk about how some wish we should embrace
and focus on caring for new immigrants over
the people who fought for our freedoms.
Seems to me that our veterans deserve superior
treatment to all; they risked their lives and left
their families, and many came back physically
or mentally damaged. They did their part to
serve our country in the service and now is the
time for them to get the benefits coming to
them. I am no expert, but Marty Burbank is,
and I would urge you to call him or others with
knowledge of veterans benefits to help you and
your family. Marty runs the Orange County
Elder Law Firm and, from all that I know, is a

man of honor. While I have never used him, and cannot recommend anyone that I have not personally worked with, if this was my issue, I would call several attorneys, meet with them, including Marty, and then choose. Marty's number is (714) 525-4600. Tell him David S. sent you.

7. **The car.** This is going to be tough. Most seniors think they are fine drivers. In many cases, unfortunately, this is not true. The car is the ultimate symbol of freedom and independence, especially for males, and there has never been a good alternative, until now. The other day I was waiting for an Uber next to an older lady who was also waiting for one. She was the first older person I had ever met who uses Uber. We had a quick talk about it, and she admitted that her family had taken away her car after she had repeated mystery scratches on her car, and her curb looked like she had hit it several times, which she had. Instead of her being dependent on them, they got her an Uber account and she loved it. No more car payments. No more gas stations. No

more repair shops. She went wherever she wanted, whenever she wanted, and her son paid for everything. She called it liberating. She donated her car to a veteran's organization in honor of her late husband, which was poetic to me. I wanted to talk more, but her car came and she was off with a wave and a smile.

These preparations for the move may sound minor, but they are not. When you have to do all of them at once, under pressure of a move, they can become overwhelming. They do not have to be. Examination of these issues may prove more important than you or they think, but if it is done correctly, they will not only reduce the stress of the move but provide the opportunity to learn more about your relatives and their lives, and may even cause a deepening respect and appreciation for all they have done and been through.

Chapter 17
SECRET SAUCE

This chapter teaches how to identify superior senior living simply by observing the staff and using the secret signs I will reveal to figure out if it is a staff-centric or senior-centric operation. My belief is that, as counterintuitive as it sounds, a staff-centric operation is much better at taking care of seniors than a senior-centric operation. Simply put, happy employees make for happy residents. Everyone preaches this, but few practice it. This chapter will also provide a playbook for owners of companies to learn how to use happiness as a profit booster and secret staffing weapon. These concepts seem inconsistent but, in reality, are not. This chapter has a twist, as it will appear, at first blush, to be backward in both structure and message. Allow me to explain.

What should you be looking for when you walk into an SL or AL building or call one on the phone? Professionally trained people who respond beautifully and make you feel warm and fuzzy? Maybe, but that is not what I want you to focus on. I want you to seek a place where the residents *and the staff* are outwardly happy, and I will provide clues as to how to determine if the latter is true or not.

> **SPOILER ALERT**: This is the single most important element of finding a new place that is right for you and the family. Remember, buildings are simply wood, wire, and metal, and you are placing a beloved person in one. Do not choose the building; do not focus on location, although that is important. Choose the culture, and choose the one with employees who are happy because they likely will make you and your family happy. You become a reflection of whom you spend time with.

This chapter is also going to take you deep into my mind as an employer. I will share my secrets here in hopes that it will not only help you find the right place but also that senior-living industry people will read this and know there is a way other than the cold, soulless, corporate-care model I have seen. Perhaps, together, we can change this culture from the inside out. So let me take you with me on the journey that changed everything quite by accident.

As a longtime employee who became an employer, initially there was a huge struggle within me. On one hand, having been an employee for many years, I believed it was crystal clear what motivated me and my other coworkers to want to be great at our jobs. However, as an employer, it was equally clear that what I wanted as an employee was very different than what I wanted as an employer. As an employee, I wanted desirable assignments, recognition, respect, promotion, appreciation, and money. As an employer, I wanted staff to work their hardest, follow directions, understand goals, solve problems, and go above and beyond the call of duty. And I did not want to break the bank with payroll costs.

When the transformation from employee to employer began, instincts took me into a conflicted and defensive posture. Being too friendly was out. Being mean and scary was effective but not sustainable. Playing favorites in my mind was justified. Playing favorites in reality was toxic.

While attending an SL conference, I joined a small breakout session in which the topic was how to get the most out of employees. The only thing that lives in my memory from that speech was one line uttered by the speaker, a VIP from a huge corporate SL entity: **"Remember that at the end of the day all the people who work for you are *paid enemies*, so treat them accordingly and cautiously."**

179

The statement shocked me. Recognizing that I was relatively unsophisticated and new to this, my first inclination was to question if this was true. Perhaps I had been looking at this challenge all wrong. I went back to my community and soon became "David the Hun." I was cold and cautious, and there was no give in me. Soon it became clear that this style did not work for me, and I entertained the thought that maybe I was not cut out for this role.

On top of everything, I had just had a very dejecting moment. When the pressure of my responsibilities felt like it was starting to choke me, I would disengage from the chaos and take a walk around the community, up and down all the stairs, and usually end up on the roof for some silence and fresh air. It gave me a chance to breathe and remember that this was just one building in a sea of buildings, in one city of a land with a thousand cities. It was my time to gain much-needed perspective.

One such day, in the middle of all of this self-doubt, I spotted a kitchen worker with a backpack walk out of the back door to the alley on his way home. Nothing unusual, except I had happened to have been in the parking lot in the morning when he had come to work and, by chance, noticed he was carrying an empty backpack at the time in his hand. Now, however, the backpack seemed full. What was now in it? It hit me that perhaps one of the reasons my food costs were so high was that people were stealing from me. My father had warned me to pay attention to such matters.

I flew down the stairs, slammed open the door to the alley, and intercepted him. When I popped out, he looked scared. I asked him how his day was and what was going on. He forced a smile and said everything was fine and said "bye" and walked past me. As he did, I eyeballed the backpack from up close. I called him by his first name and asked, "Why is your backpack bleeding?"

He acted like he no longer knew English. I pointed to the blood dripping from his backpack. I extended my hand. He handed me the backpack. When I unzipped it, the backpack was packed with huge and expensive meats. To make it worse, the month before, he had been named my employee of the month. I felt stupid and deeply betrayed.

Once a month, my father, Jack, would drive to see me and take me out to lunch to take my psychological temperature. He barely had a high-school education but was the smartest man I have ever known. Incredible instincts. He simply understood people. After sharing the story of the conference, the bloody backpack, and the long list of my failures, I admitted I did not know what to do anymore. The community was financially struggling, residents were complaining, I was the new leader, staff was stealing, and the pressure to succeed was suffocating me. There was no sleep or rest at night. An impasse had been reached, and I lacked his vision. "What should I do, Dad?"

"Just be yourself, David," he said with a smile. "Because if you are anyone else you will not be believable. People have to trust and believe in you, and if you do not believe in yourself, then no one will ever follow you."

The total faith and trust I had in him cannot be communicated here in words, so, simply put, I accepted his words 100 percent. **That advice became the Jack Slomovic Doctrine (JSD).** By deciding to live this doctrine, I felt an immediate release of anxiety and fear, as there was no more doubt or trying to be whom I thought they needed or wanted. It was an awkward and arranged marriage, but we were going to make it work.

What came out of all this was what people eventually referred to as our "secret sauce." It was very simple. Being myself meant trusting my instincts, leading with my heart, and reacting as I had been raised by my parents. My goal was to take care of the people who were taking care of my people. In other words, taking great care of my staff so that they would take great care of my residents. There was no playbook I had read—and I had read many—that effectively communicated a system that actually worked. I had experimented with dozens of systems and twists to systems, but, in the end, we needed all hands rowing together, and it seemed impossible.

Until I stopped trying. When I stopped trying and gave up on the idea that I had or could acquire all the answers to uncover the secret to perfect staffing, I just waved the white flag of pretending to know everything. And then it happened, completely by accident.

It began with a heartbreaking call. My chef, who ended up working with me for nearly seventeen of my eighteen years there, was very much my right hand. The kitchen and food are critical, as you know by now, and the chef makes you look good or makes you look bad. We had a strong bond, although, at times, he would only do things his way. He used to say, "David, you take care of the front, and I got the back." Keep in mind he was responsible for approximately 1,100 meals being served every month. We had sparred multiple times, but, as my father used to ask, "Are *you* going to cook for one hundred and twenty people three times a day?" Chef was a pro, and I trusted and respected him. We made a formidable team.

So when one day my longtime assistant, Dorothy, walked in with big doe eyes looking like the world had just exploded, I was not sure what to expect. She, almost in a whisper, told me that Chef had gone to the VA for a medical checkup, they found something bad, and he was on an operating table having emergency bypass surgery right then. It was unclear if he would survive.

My heart was in my throat. He was an hour away at the VA. I got in the car and drove there. When I arrived, it was windy, dark, and raining. I lied to the guard and said I was his son and snuck through the empty hospital and cautiously asked where he was, praying that they would not say the morgue. I was directed to a quiet part of ICU, and the nurse on shift told me it was touch and go and that I might want to say anything I wanted to say now, even though he was highly medicated and unconscious and would not hear a word I was going to say. The nurse patted me on the back to console me, and I realized this might be the last time I would ever see him.

Going to the hospital was not a calculated move or strategy. I simply cared about him and was heartbroken. When I found him, he had so many tubes coming out of him, I could not process it. He looked weak and beyond sedated, and it was shocking to see someone who was always so strong now look weak and defenseless. At first,

I sat there wondering about life and if he was going to live through the night. Then I realized the impact, selfishly, that losing him would have on me and the operations. I knew intellectually that everyone was replaceable, of course, but Chef was simply irreplaceable.

I decided to talk to him. It was like talking to a plant. Zero response. I wiped tears from my eyes as I told him how much I needed him and how sick and tired I was of his crap (Chef would have appreciated the gallows humor). I told him he needed to get up and back into my kitchen, and that we were having lasagna tomorrow, and who the hell was going to cook it. I went on and on and told him he was going to make it through the night and get back to Sunnycrest, back to the residents who need him and back to driving me crazy. I told him I need him to stop being sick and such a selfish SOB and…gurgle…he flinched, opened his eye, looked at me, and started moaning and reaching for me. I just about pooped my pants. The nurse ran in and shot something into his IV. Chef looked right at me, closed his eyes, and was out again.

I was clutching my chest and hyperventilating. The nurse asked if I was okay and I yelled *no*. After that, we decided I should leave. It was going to be a long recovery at best, she told me. When I got outside again, the rain and wind reflected my mood perfectly.

That night, I drove to my father's home and told him everything. We discussed finding a replacement, but he told me to not replace Chef. He told me to eat the overtime and bring in extra help but to keep Chef on staff and on the payroll at full pay. This made no sense to me. He could not cook, could not do the ordering, could not train or do anything, and if I listened to the medical people, he likely would not even survive.

"Pay him his regular salary and call his wife and tell her what you are going to do." He explained that Chef was a proud man whose number-one concern was taking care of his family. He needed to know they would be okay so that he could recover without the pressure of trying to rush back. We argued about the practicality of this, but there was no debating with my father once he had made up his mind.

Arrangements were made, staffing was beefed up, and overtime eaten. I spoke to his wife and invited her to stay at our home, which was close to the hospital so she did not have to do that drive in her state of mind. She could not believe it.

This was the JSD in action.

It worked. Months later, Chef slowly but triumphantly walked back into his kitchen and worked for us for another ten or twelve years until the day we sold! You have never seen anyone as happy as Chef the day he walked back into our community, or a group of people happier to see someone. He was greeted like MacArthur returning to the Philippines. After so many years of Chef taking care of us with such loyalty, Chef had become family.

And that was our "secret sauce." We, or I (after my father passed away), treated wonderful and loyal staff like family.

What does this mean? It means that you take care of people and treat them the way you want to be treated. What does it mean and what does it actually look like? And does it all come down to money? Most of the time, no.

Unusual and extreme exceptions, like the Chef situation, do exist. For example, one day I noticed that a certain longtime employee had suddenly cashed out all of her vacation. She worked in the kitchen, so I pulled Chef aside and asked if anything was going on.

"You caught that, huh?" was his response. Turns out she needed an operation and was going to pay for it out-of-pocket. Despite her wages and vacation, she was still $1,000 short, he told me.

"She has family, they will pool their money, and she will be fine."

Next payroll, I slipped an extra $1,000 check into her envelope. I added a note, "Get better soon." I was walking out of the building when she caught up to me. She hugged and kissed me so hard I thought I was going to snap in two.

"Just get better soon. We need you," I told her.

She was crying. She had the operation and came back and continued to be wonderful to our residents and worked for us for years until we sold. This was not a planned or calculated move. It was simply helping someone who had been loyal and sweet to my residents for years. It just seemed like the right thing to do.

Our executive director was severely injured after being attacked by a lunatic. I took her place until she recovered and came back to work. Again, we paid her the full salary even though she did not work for nearly half a year. Without an ED, much like being without a chef, the very heart and soul of the operations are missing. She was single and had no other form of income or family help, and she was traumatized by the attack. She ultimately came back, and although she was a very unemotional lady, she cried and told me no one would have done this for her and that, frankly, she did not even understand why we did it. I did, of course. Years later, when her performance became nonexistent, and she needed to be replaced, she was still grateful and commented on what we had done for her.

She was right. No one else would have done this for her. And, truth be told, I do not think it was all about the money. I think it was about caring for people when they can no longer help you. We had no idea if any of these three would bounce back and return. It was not about talking the talk. It was about walking the walk when there had been no talk.

These are heartwarming examples of the Jack Slomovic Doctrine. But they are only an extreme of the JSD spectrum, in which loyalty cost significant funds. But the JSD is not about throwing money at things; it is about paying attention to people. For example, one day, the chef was on a roll, thrilled at how his beloved New York Giants were doing. A native New Yorker, Chef loved his Giants and even his Giants coffee mug. Later that year, I got him and his wife good tickets to see the Giants play in San Diego. That meant a lot to him. It showed I noticed what he said.

Here's another example of how doing this is not financially costly. Weeks before the sale of my company closed, I was leaving the building and spotted a staff member on the street riding her bike without a helmet. A lovely young mother of two small children, I made a mental note of it as I drove away. The next day, I asked Chef why she did not wear one.

"Helmets cost money," was his blunt response. So I had my assistant purchase a helmet and place it in her locker. She could not believe not only that I noticed, but that I cared enough to go through the effort and expense to put her safety as a priority in my busy life. When I eventually saw her in person, I reminded her how important she was and how much she needed to take care of herself, especially now that she has the two little ones. Her wonderful smile and twinkling eyes warmed my heart, but her safety was my real reward. The irony of all of this is that, by doing these acts for people, one cannot help but feel happy and good inside, and people feel and sense that.

These actions were not designed to produce anything else for me. They were simply gestures of love, respect, and goodwill. There was no clear return on investment, and, in most cases, the expenditure of money was probably illogical. But it was moral, and it was right, and it was what allowed people to heal, or that made them feel good, or that simply showed that I cared or was paying attention. At its core, we put wonderful people ahead of profits, only to later discover that by doing so, we became more profitable by getting committed leadership, avoiding turnover, and breeding a warm culture of belonging. And that is the ultimate key. Everyone in life, I sincerely believe, wants most of all to be understood, and to be appreciated for who they are, not just what they do for you. By going beyond what anyone would expect, by showing that every person matters, by caring about the health and safety of others when you have no responsibility to do so, that is the true measure of who you are. That is the true measure of leadership. That is what I learned from my father. That, my friends, was our secret sauce. True caring.

You cannot force it. You cannot fake it. You cannot bottle it. But when it is real, people will know it and feel it and take a bullet for you. They will come in to work that double shift even when they have plans if someone calls out at the last minute. They will leave a wedding in a tuxedo to come help with a flood, and they will take care of your people with a smile and a full heart.

And therein lies the **happiness advantage**. By making our people happy for the sake of them being happy, they felt appreciated and respected and were motivated to work their hardest, understand our goals, solved problem, and go above and beyond the call of duty. They viewed *our* success as *their* success. Of the things mentioned here, while not cheap, did not break the bank or even come close. They probably even saved money. We invested in our employees' happiness, and the results spoke for themselves.

In fact, most of these actions had virtually little cost. My ED once expressed frustration at the constant turnover, personality issues, and conflicts within the caregiving department. This disharmony not only causes expensive overtime but often leads to sudden and unexplained job abandonment or even phantom worker's compensation claims. So I invited the caregivers to meet with me so I could get to know them better and diagnose the source of the problem. The evening and overnight staff are rarely seen and need some face time, too.

Gathering for pizza and soda, we went around the table between bites. I asked them why they did this work. Each one had a personal story about being drawn to caring of others. Usually, it was taking care of a specific family member they loved. Woman after woman cried upon recounting whom it was they cared for. They released their hidden truth, and we all bonded that night. This element, by the way, of having tripped into this industry because they had cared for someone they loved, was one of the hidden elements that I looked for during the critical interviewing process. These are the people who do this for the right reasons, who have open and giving hearts and see this as their calling. As their mission. Those are the people I want working for me in my organization.

After the pizza and the talk and hugs, the entire caregiving department bonded and made peace, and at least for a while, all the problems went away. Cost me a couple of pizzas and a couple of hours. I got to know these ladies and what made them tick. Most did not even know each other's stories. It is amazing how hard these ladies work and what situations they come from. They should be admired. Time and effort and forty dollars very well spent.

What is the cost of not paying attention? The biggest hidden killer of an operation is staff turnover. The ads. The calls. The interviews. The fingerprints. The waiting. The training. All to see if they even know how to swim in these seas.

Earlier in the chapter, I mentioned I would provide clues to see if the staff was happy or not, and urged you to choose the happy staff. What are the clues? This chapter has struck a deep nerve in me, and that is reflected in the amount of space given to it. So I will end this chapter here and share the clues in the next chapter. The overarching message here is that the JSD is about being the king or queen that the staff would choose if they had the choice. It's about having the strength, wisdom, and insight to know what to do, and to go above and beyond expectations to give people what they need even if they did not even know what was missing. They in turn (if you pick the right people), will do the same for your residents. That is the dynamic the right culture creates, and this is 90 percent of the battle.

Chapter 18
SECRET SIGNS

What are the signs of a happy staff?

As simple as it sounds, look for staff that smiles. I must have mystery shopped one hundred AL communities in my day, and what struck me over and over again was the lack of smiles or a happy vibe when I first walked in. Observe the residents in the lobby. Look at their faces. Did they look bored, sad, or are they asleep?

Then look to the staff. Are the staff engaged and speaking with the residents? Or are they walking around, heads down, going from place to place like robots? Does the receptionist stand up, smile, and extend a hand when you walk in? Or does he or she avoid eye contact or even hold up a finger for you to wait until the end of a phone call? Worse yet, does the receptionist ignore you?

Where is the leadership? AL ownership and leadership generally like to keep a healthy distance from the staff and residents. But the impact of an ED or owner sitting in the dining room having a meal with a group of residents is astronomical. It sends a strong and positive message to all residents, even if the ED is only hearing complaints, but to the residents and most families who might see it, this is pure gold. But the biggest impact is on the staff itself. They see that the owner or director cares, is paying attention to what they do, and is not afraid to engage.

As you walk around the communities you are considering, look to see if most of the managers and leaders are sitting in their offices, or if they out with the residents checking things and learning what is working and what is not. Ninety percent of the time, managers are sitting in their offices, which tells me they are not engaged or doing serious reconnaissance or problem solving. How do staff and residents interact with your tour leader. Does the leader know everyone by name?

Does the tour leader ask a resident a personal question like "Myrtle, how did bridge go today?" Or ask about the family member who just visited? Does the tour leader address the staff? Do the staff make eye contact and smile, or do they hide? These secret signs are an indicator of what you are heading into—better to understand what is going on now before you make the move.

Perhaps you think that this is fluff. That it reflects ego and not observation.

That would be a fair observation.

Recently, a former employee called to see how I was doing. I was writing this book at the time, and while I had them on the phone, I asked how, in hindsight, they felt about Sunnycrest's culture how they perceived my leadership style now that I was gone and would no longer be signing their checks. The response was that the staff felt loved and that they mattered. That they had worked many other places but never felt what they felt there, before or since. That if they had a personal problem they could come to me. That in most places the leaders avoid interacting with staff and residents. That I was a visible leader and therefore a strong one. That staff who are cared about are happy and create a warm environment for the residents. That it was not about money. That staff feeling cared for in the "little things" (pizza lunches, zip line excursions). That being made to feel important is not about money but about a warm sense of belonging.

Then there are the secret signs about the building itself. You want to see if people enjoy going to the meals in the dining room. Are the halls littered with room service trays? If yes, then either you have a lot of people who do not want to come to the dining hall (bad sign), or are currently sick (also a bad sign, but it happens). Is the parking lot full of cars? If yes, then you likely have active residents versus those who have eliminated the costs and stresses of vehicle ownership. Are the doors decorated? If yes, then you're likely to have more engaged residents and families. Does the community even allow that? That is a philosophical question that also reflects ideals.

What is the cleanliness level? Do you see staff cleaning? God forbid, are there offensive smells? While this is part of life there, it should be taken care of by the time you walk back that way.

When you walk through the halls, peek into nonpublic areas and into resident apartments. How is the cleanliness of the apartment? Do they seem well taken care of? This is, by the way, an opportunity to eavesdrop on staff interacting with residents. What is the tone? Warm? Friendly? This is where you find out what you can expect once the checks are cashed, and the marketing love is in the rearview mirror.

Are they hyping brain games and complex anti-Alzheimer's computer spaces and/or gyms? This is often the case with the bigger companies, and they explain how these cognitive and physical exercises keep you strong longer. It is a powerful message, but I have never seen anyone in these spaces, and when I see a resident actually doing it, it will be the first time.

Does the staff look you in the eyes and smile and say hello as you pass them in the halls? That is a sign they are robotic and going through the motions. They are most likely unhappy, not engaged, and have not bought into the bigger mission.

Longevity is the other big clue as to whether the staff is happy. Someone who is happy stays. Someone who is unhappy leaves. At the time of the sale, Chef had been with me around seventeen years, my maintenance supervisor fifteen, and my ED almost six. This was not an accident, and it was not unusual for the rank and file to have been there five to ten years, if not longer. The final point on the cheat sheet is whether or not multiple family members work there. I loved employing multiple family members because they were more invested in the business.

Let your eyes tell you the story. If the staff has energy and pep and seem happy to be there, and thus happy to see you, they likely are happy and want you to move in and be a part of it. That means there is a positive culture there. If they stay for years, and they have family working there, this place jumps to the front of the line. You can ask some questions like, "How long have you worked here?" If there are two staff members, smile and ask, "Is this your sister?" If you hear "No, but my sister works in the kitchen," then you know you have scored.

The happiness of the residents is closely related to staff happiness, and in fact, the same exact practices apply. Every leader should walk the halls as often as possible. It is shocking how many stay hidden, safe, and unreachable in their offices. In walking around, observations are made organically. Spotting a resident struggling with a room key, I would get on my walkie-talkie and have a maintenance guy run over before the resident even knew I was there. The joy in the eyes of the resident of not even having to ask for help was pure gold. I heard a resident calling for her cat over and over, so I knocked on the door to see if she was okay. She told me she had to take her cat to the vet and had no idea how she was going to do it. I offered to get her a cat carrier as a present. She declined, but it was as if I had offered her a limo to the Oscars. It is all about being seen and heard. The cost? Zero dollars.

We had residents leave, of course, but almost never because they were unhappy. Yes, some difficult and/or dishonest people came and went. Good riddance. The vast majority of my residents were happy. Not only that, but, in the end, I had residents who volunteered to give marketing tours to potential residents. Nothing was more powerful than a resident senior giving a tour to another senior and/or their family explaining why they were so happy. This touches again on the massive importance of residents having a purpose, but in this context, we had finally achieved the dream of all hands rowing together. With the happiness advantage in full force, we achieved tremendous growth and success and reached the highest financial heights in the history of the company.

This tenor was perfectly summed up in a letter by my ED, who resigned his position the day after I announced the sale of the community. He told me later that he only wanted to work for the Slomovic Family.

In the letter, he wrote, "I have been inspired by the results we have achieved with respect to seeing senior citizens become so much happier and healthier in the most majestic ways through exercise, socialization, nutrition and creating an optimal professional team of motivated and compassionate employees.

"Sunnycrest has given me a great canvas over the last period of years to help paint an extraordinary environment where seniors not only thrive but they also come back to life bringing deep emotional joy and happiness to their beloved family members."

This articulate message deeply affected me. When was the last time you repeatedly saw the word "happiness" written, and this type of soul, in a letter of resignation?

I have now given you the secret signs to look for and what they mean.

However, my friends, there is a massive problem on the SL horizon. The staffing problems of motivation and focus on the mission are very real. They affect the enjoyment you or your family will experience. The people working must be engaged and nurtured for maximum effectiveness. But there are more buildings being built and more companies being formed as everyone runs as fast as they can into what they see as the money pit of elder care due to the aging baby boomers. The problem is there is no pipeline creating these ideal employees, and with more facilities and seniors right around the corner, having happy and effective staff is more important than ever.

The people problem is real, and there are not enough well-trained and screened employees to fulfill the staffing demands projected for the aging baby boomer population. This "Silver Tsunami" is coming, and the SL world is standing on the beach with an expensive company-branded umbrella staring into this megawave. SL is unprepared from not only a numbers point of view but also a quality point of view.

Labor got easy in 2009. But high turnover rates, low morale, a shortage of bodies, wage pressures, a lack of leadership flow, and rising costs have not only had a negative impact on resident satisfaction, but are also forming the perfect storm for the future. This is especially true in California, where minimum wages hit a whopping fifteen dollars an hour. Do you think that is going to impact your costs? You'd better believe it. The "people problem" is real and soon to hit the industry smack in the face like a frozen fish.

So to combat this, most, if not all, in the industry are grasping at ways to keep their good people, find new ways to recruit and retain talent, and keep costs from spiraling out of control. In a nutshell, brands are struggling to find people who want to do this difficult work, which tends not to pay well, and mostly to keep from fighting over the same small group of people. If you can make fifteen dollars an hour wiping down tables or making coffee, are you going to clean adult diapers and bathe the elderly for those same fifteen dollars? Think about it.

Ironically, two days ago, I listened to a webinar on the topic of "Building a Senior Living Organization Where Teams Love Coming to Work." The usual talk of mission, vision, and values rang hollow to me, but the element of trying to increase employee satisfaction caught my ear. One company focused on what is essentially branding to attract *employees* instead of *customers*. They discussed specially designed staffing clothing (with staff input), and fancy employee lounges with Ping-Pong tables and air hockey in the front of the building instead of relegated to the back.

I shook my head listening to all this because, while it may work, to me, it misses the boat. It fails to comprehend the core motivation of these employees. These people do not need "stuff" at work. They want to be seen. They want to be understood. They want to care for others and to be cared for.

They do not do this difficult work simply for a check. They are drawn to help people, and specifically the elderly, these often lonely and vulnerable seniors, and are not doing it purely for the money. It is their calling. That needs to be appreciated. That needs to be understood. That is the way to have happy employees, and happy employees made magically happy residents, and relieved and content families.

Respectfully, employee happiness is not about a Ping-Pong table. Someone else can always get a better trick. It is about the soul.

But perhaps they are right and I am wrong. Perhaps I am too "old school" to keep up with what drives young people, and I, too, am part of the past. Perhaps "Googlizing" SL employment is the missing piece of the giant puzzle. But I do not think so, at least not long-term. The seminal moment of the webinar came when I heard something that brought a smile to my face: "No one can figure out the secret sauce to having good employee satisfaction."

You sure about that?

Chapter 19
SENIORS GONE WILD

Earlier, I explained that many negatives exist in terms of how we as a society view seniors. What might surprise you is how seniors see themselves. The negative view on seniors and aging is not shared by seniors at all. And they are beginning to fight back in unrecognized, unanticipated, and sometimes less than positive ways. Hence, seniors gone wild.

What do I mean? I mean that seniors are smart and on the clock and know they are being marginalized. Their responses may shock you. They shock me. These ways may surprise you and even disturb you, and maybe melt your mind a little, so do not say I did not warn you.

First off, this chapter is being written within months of the conclusion of the 2016 presidential election. No matter who you wanted to win or what you believe, one thing popped out at me over and over, but almost no one said a single word about it.

The White House and age. Despite the extreme amount of coverage and the seemingly endless political presidential cycle, there was an important hidden fact that virtually no one directly spoke about or paid any attention to. That silent issue was the relatively older ages of the major party candidates. Despite all the attention and politicking on social media and talk about whether the millennials would vote and whether younger people care was a very fascinating twist. Hillary Clinton, at the time of the vote, was sixty-eight years old, and Donald Trump was seventy. This became relevant when a video of a swaying, buckling Hillary Clinton at a 9/11 event came to light. Suddenly rumors about her health exploded, and questions as to whether she was "too old" for the job came up. This became an extra touchy subject because Trump is slightly older than Clinton, bringing up the issue of male versus female aging related to physical demands, as well as mental acuity required for the biggest and most important job in the world.

FiveThirtyEight, a fascinating and popular political/sports website, devoted an article to the subject. "Can a Candidate Be Too Old to Run for President?" was published in September 2016 and debated this very issue. Was this fair game with candidates whose combined ages totaled 138?

The reality is that, when Trump took over the White House in January of 2017, he was the oldest person ever elected for their first term as president. Hillary Clinton would have tied the current record holder, Ronald Reagan, who was sixty-nine, and had she taken office, she would have been twenty-two years older than her husband, former president Bill Clinton, had been when he took office. What does this mean? Is this fair game? This is an especially fascinating question considering that the forty-fourth and outgoing president, Barack Obama, took office at age forty-seven, making him the fourth youngest after Teddy Roosevelt (forty-two), JFK (forty-three), Bill Clinton (forty-six), and Ulysses S. Grant (forty-six). What does it say that the forty-fifth will now be the oldest or that, for the highest most important office of the land, both parties picked senior citizens? Also, is there pushback from the older generation fighting to stay in power, or have people concluded that experience and accomplishments do matter?

Add to that the fascinating Bernie Sanders phenomenon. Bernie was a nondescript and relatively unknown Vermont senator who came out of nowhere to challenge Hillary Clinton and become her chief competitor for the nomination. Sanders, at the ripe old age of seventy-five, drew large crowds, and his populist message found a massive following, especially among the under-forty crowd, who embraced and loved the "Feel the Bern" slogan. Sanders, who very nearly upended Clinton, would have been the oldest American president ever.

What does it say that the three top picks for the presidency all are somewhat advanced senior citizens? What does it say that many of the followers of each are the young? Why is the message of a better future resonating exclusively from the old? Or was it all just pure coincidence?

This question is an intriguing one, but most snapshots I am seeing about seniors do not relate to incredible achievement or society praising them. Quite the opposite. They are of seniors who need help or just do not care anymore.

There is a dark side to seniors refusing to go gently into that good night. One of the most touchy and complex issues of aging is driving—specifically, when to pull the plug on a senior keeping the keys to that multi-ton four-wheeled missile when they still possess a valid license, but their abilities have declined. Most seniors would rather be shot than lose their vehicle and thus their independence and freedom.

I recall a couple from Alabama who lived in my community. A proud and devoted father and husband, the gentlemen dressed in a suit almost daily and treated his wife like a queen. But when dementia started to make its way into his mind, everything went sideways.

I remember a day when he drove up to the community, parked his car, got out, and walked in. Nothing unusual except that he had parked the car smack in the middle of the street. When I walked out to see why he did this, he said hello and walked right past me. Taken aback, I asked why he had parked that way. He had no idea what I was talking about. When I showed him the car placement, he asked me why *I* had done such a thing. He had no idea he had done it. This was the beginning of the end of his stay at my place, as we were not designed for this situation, but what struck me the most was when I felt I had to call his family and tell them there had been a change in his condition and what he had done. They asked me what to do. I suggested they call the DMV and ask for him to be retested. He did and he failed, and they took the car soon after. He did not remember exactly what had happened, but he blamed me and told me that taking away his car was the most evil thing I could have done to him. Men's identity, in particular, is wrapped around their cars and their ability to have instant freedom. That is not something to take lightly.

This may be the touchiest of all subjects, but it also feels like a week does not go by without a story of a senior losing control of a vehicle or needing assistance. I remember hearing about an old man who lost control of his car and killed people at the Santa Monica Farmers

Market. He never intended for that to happen. But the damage was done.

Here are some examples of seniors stubbornly holding on to their world by their fingernails or being in need of police or other help because they have overestimated their abilities, do not realize they have lost their edge, or do not care anymore.

I kept a list for a couple of weeks. Keep in mind I do not surf the Internet daily or watch much TV, and I rarely watch the news, so the ratio of sites I looked at and the bizarre stories on seniors was disproportionately high.

Story number one related to senior truck drivers and how some may be responsible for a significant upswing in crashes and deaths on the highways. One show I caught by chance said that many drivers are not only in their seventies and eighties, but some are still driving in their nineties! They have valid licenses and passed the tests, but when is enough *enough*? Terrifying.

Second story was about a Santa Fe police officer who saved the life of an eighty-seven-year-old lady. She was had been driving on a flat tire, which caused the car to catch fire. The car was engulfed in flames and the cab full of smoke when he pulled her out. He even "retrieved her cane."

The third was a horrible story about an older couple in Los Feliz, who were attacked and robbed in their home. The robbers, whom the wife believed had worked in their home as contractors, harmed and struck the elderly couple when they resisted giving up their jewelry and watch. The wife said she was angry and frustrated and felt they had been targeted because they are seniors and live alone.

I have saved the worst for last. Sex. Yes, as disturbing as this may sound, sex and seniors apparently now mix, in some cases far too much. Viagra and Celeste have found their place in the aging world. While in commercials you see the forty-five to sixty-year-old couple prancing around as the man with gray hair cautiously looks at her, and she confidently leads him around their vacation villa or boat, nothing could be further from the truth. Like nearly everything, that is pure marketing spin. The reality is that the ones taking that stuff, from what I hear and have been told, are mostly bald seventy- or eighty-plus men sitting around at bingo.

I have heard of communities, particularly in Florida, where STDs are the number-one health issue and, frankly, out of control. One was the subject of a reality TV show whose name I cannot recall. It was a somewhat disturbing, somewhat uplifting, window into how younger seniors live. They exhibited behavior that was very much like high school, except everyone was over sixty-five. It was almost as if they realize the clock was ticking and they were going to try to go back in time to do everything they had always wanted to do, along with everything they were doing before when they were younger. Kind of like *Bucket List* meets *Back to the Future*. They want it all, and then some.

These communities are for more active and somewhat younger seniors, but one story I heard said that the local physicians requested discussions with the seniors regarding rampant sexual activity and STDs. Turns out that the little blue pills are like crack for seniors, and they love it. The problem, apparently, is that the ratio of men to women in most communities is disproportionately female, leading to immense popularity among the men.

In a very small way, we saw this at my community once, where two ladies got into a shouting match in the dining room at lunch. Seems they were fighting over this one gentlemen. One lady was his girlfriend and the other was, let's call her, a "new friend." When one confronted the other, a yelling match broke out, with very inappropriate language being used by both ladies. I went over to see what I could do. The ladies were standing there like they were about to get violent. I was shocked. I walked in and stood between them trying to calm everyone down and to let them know this type of disturbance was not going to go on in my building. But they ignored me. These were the two most vocal and negative ladies in the entire building, and watching them square off took me so by surprise I was speechless. My lasting memory was glancing at the man they were fighting over, and seeing the largest smile I have ever seen.

Yes, seniors do still get jiggy with it. But, honestly, for every one of these situations, the much more normal situation is that residents find other residents to sit and have meals with, sometimes of the opposite sex, and this pleasant companionship is more than enough to fill their cup. These wild older people, thirsting for the zest of young life, are the outliers, and outliers by a country mile.

These are examples of seniors refusing to budge or accept the sands of time, or give up even one more inch to aging. They are going to die with their boots on *their way*, and some have suggested it is not about seniors gone wild, but seniors gone crazy. I think it truly is neither.

These seniors realize that time is no longer on their side, and they weigh the risks and rewards of their choices, except now much of the risk is gone and has evaporated for them. They perceive, I sense, that they have little to nothing to lose anymore. Some have flatly told me they are not afraid to die. They are not tempered by worrying about another forty years remaining. They are not living for or held back by their original spouse or, in many cases, even their second spouse. They are the lemonade generation, and may have the greatest adaptation skills of all.

They may perceive that they only have lemons left, but they sure as hell are not going to cry about it. They never have and they are not about to start now. They are going to make the best out of the situation as they always have because this is who they are. And the one thing no one can take away from seniors is self-perception of their identity, and when it comes right down to it, no one ever should. This, however, must be tempered by reason and potential risks to others. Thankfully, we are on the cusp of perhaps the greatest positive for seniors (since Viagra). Self-driving cars may soon inhabit America, and thankfully this could prove huge for the ever-growing senior population.

In the end, it is a mixed bag of facts. The seniors of today are, and are viewed as, a dichotomy. On one hand, they are recognized and followed leaders. They have accumulated wealth and wisdom. Their "seniority" has a lot to offer, as reflected in whom we chose to be presidential candidates.

But their vast knowledge and experience can also be a practical negative. The other day I was driving, and one car was slower than all the others. People honked aggressively and changed lanes until they passed the slow car. I eventually changed lanes, and as I passed, I glanced over. Barely visible was an old woman in a hat with fake flowers. Probably less than five feet tall, she could barely see over the dashboard. She had fiercely focused eyes forward as she drove five to ten miles under the speed limit, driving perfectly straight in her lane, while everyone was driving above it. Many were honking and cursing at her, and I saw one man give her the finger. I despise that and instantly loved and admired her perfect driving.

Seems to me that, at her age, it is fair to ask if perhaps she is not still safe to drive, or perhaps we all are missing something very simple—how we process information. I am no expert, but I would guess that older people drive (and react) slower not simply because reflexes are poorer, but because they have more information from life experiences than the rest of us do. Essentially, they have more info in "storage." I could be wrong, but maybe they are slower because they have more data that they have to mentally process due to experience. Who knows? But I want to make a national suggestion. Let's stop honking at old people. It scares them, assuming they can hear it, and probably makes the overall situation more dangerous for everyone.

No one talks about any of these issues or wants to look at this part of it. I sincerely believe that everyone knows someone like this, or even in the deepest and darkest parts of their mind is secretly afraid of the day that this is actually *us*. It feels and becomes very different when we contemplate these concerns being applied to *us* instead of *them*, doesn't it? That should tell us something important.

These topics are not pretty and are uncomfortable to discuss openly. I have never seen or heard these topics mentioned or examined in the forty to fifty senior-living events and conferences I have attended. This is what we are *not* supposed to talk about. That is a part of the problem. If we are going to truly break down the walls and be honest and true to ourselves and our seniors, then we must be real if we are going to change the core of the senior-living paradigm.

Where is the path to a better, safer, happier, and less stressful way of life for them? And for us one day? How do we keep seniors from going "wild"?

The answer is potentially right in front of our faces.

We are the 90 percenters. The ones who need but ignore the SL option. Perhaps we do not realize that we can make it so good that people want to be there, are proud to be there, and thrive there. My family, just before I sold the company, joined me at our community's annual Hawaiian luau. We had island music, tropical drinks, costumed men doing wild dances, beautiful girls in coconut tops and grass skirts, yummy food, my daughters' delicious homemade cake pops, and the beautiful and timeless aloha spirit. Near the end, as the dancers finished a sequence and my youngest son was enjoying a drink, he turned to me and, with joy in his eyes, said, "Daddy, I can't wait to be old."

That is the SL world we must offer to people. The better life.

Living alone or in relative isolation, dependent on questionable and unscreened outside people or emergency government officials for assistance…is that really freedom? Is that why seniors are taking risks and living in the skin of their old lives or creating new lives? That is a different matter and a choice people are clearly free to make. If only there were an SL solution in which older people could remain themselves but live together in safety surrounded by screened, reliable, and wonderful caring people. If only that existed.

Chapter 20
RAW LAW

Earlier, I explained that I left law because practicing became increasingly unfulfilling and frustrating to me the more and more serious the cases became. It was not that I did not like the heavier cases. Truth is, they were much more interesting than the nickel-and-dime thefts, DUIs, or drug matters. Additionally, the heavier the cases, the fewer I received. So in a way, the lighter the workload. This allowed me to concentrate on more serious matters carrying more serious implications and consequences.

Just prior to starting law school in 1987, I finished an internship as a Capitol Hill legislative intern for a national organization and loved DC. It was an amazing time in America. Reagan was in office, and during the period of time I was there, Ollie North and the Iran-Contra hearings were dominating the headlines. Washington was the most vibrant playground I had ever found, and everyone I knew either was or planned on being an attorney.

Around the same time, the television show *LA Law* had debuted, and everyone wanted that cool and sleek life of the high-powered attorney. The show was funny and sexy and dealt with complex issues, and everyone wanted to be Arnie Becker, the lawyer played by Corbin

Bernsen. Little did we know that despite the associated spike in people who wanted to be attorneys, the reality of law was going to be quite different than the show.

Everything in life, I believe, is about expectations. When I was in DC. and in law school, and even watching *LA Law*, I imagined the twists and turns that awaited me. The reality was, let's just say, a little different.

Allow me to provide a specific example of the sleek and sexy life of an attorney dedicated to helping the indigent. This case was called the "Dead Dog Deaf Lady" case, and this is what actually happened.

THE DEAD DOG DEAF LADY CASE

One day I got a called to go to chambers by the judge of the courtroom I was handling. This was an unusual request. He brought me in privately and said that he needed me to do him "a solid." In other words, a favor. He had a super-tough *pro per* (defendant representing herself), and he wanted me to take the case as she was unable to properly defend herself and was driving him insane. The defendant was an older woman who loved her dogs, and one day she took one of her dogs to the vet. It was unclear exactly what had transpired medically at the vet, but, sadly, the dog passed away. The details as to how and why were sketchy, but the upshot was that she was furious and blamed the vet for the loss of her dog. She labeled him a murderer. She then started calling the vet's office multiple times a day, every day, yelling and screaming at the vet and his staff endlessly to the point of grinding the office to a halt. It appeared to be sheer harassment. He asked me to take the case.

He could not say that if I were to do this for him, he would, if he could, cut one of my clients a break in the future, but that was the implicit message, although he had total deniability. I had the opportunity to bank a get-out-of-jail-free card.

Frankly, this was pure gold, and there was no way was I going to miss this opportunity. I could see this case was going to be a nightmare, but I felt I owed it to some future client to have an ace up my sleeve. Plus, had I said no, the judge would not forget that either and make me pay by getting back at one or more of my clients in a way I could never prove. So I accepted.

I forgot to mention the key point of the picture, which the judge conveniently forgot to mention before gaining my consent. The client was deaf. Stone deaf from birth, and she could not really speak, so she would call up yelling and screaming in demented-sounding, blood-curdling shrieks and howls. It was very difficult to understand her words, as the rants were a menagerie of curses and threats and pain and vitriol, but you could make out certain words such as "killer," "murderer," and fragments like "gonna get you," if you listened closely. It was ugly on every level, and I could understand why the vet would push for prosecution.

The vet initially did not know what to do. He had figured she would run out of steam and go away. He was wrong. She did not. The calls kept coming, and eventually she started to strangle his office. He did not know what to do, so he called the city attorney's office and complained. The CA tracked the calls to her home phone and recorded her rants. They must have had over one hundred calls tracked and taped before they felt they had enough, and they had a restraining order that had been filed as well. Based on these elements, they charged her with over one hundred counts of section 422 of the Penal Code, Making Terrorist Threats. Although they were misdemeanors based on the volume and how they were charged, she was potentially looking at years in jail.

I had never had a case with this charge before, and because it was in the 1990s (pre-9/11), terrorist threats had a very different meaning back then. I loved the challenge of it but needed to do mass amounts of research.

Section 422: Any person who willfully threatens to commit a crime which will result in death or great bodily injury to another person, with the specific intent that the statement, made verbally, in writing, or by means of an electronic communication device, is to be taken as a threat, even if there is no intent of actually carrying it out, which, on its face and under the circumstances in which it is made, is so unequivocal, unconditional, immediate, and specific as to convey to the person threatened, a gravity of purpose and an immediate prospect of execution of the threat, and thereby causes that person reasonably to be in sustained fear for his or her own safety or for his or her immediate family's safety, shall be punished by imprisonment in the county jail not to exceed one year, or by imprisonment in the state prison.

For the purposes of this section, "immediate family" means any spouse, whether by marriage or not, parent, child, any person related by consanguinity or affinity within the second degree, or any other person who regularly resides in the household, or who, within the prior six months, regularly resided in the household.

Electronic communication device:

This includes, but is not limited to, telephones, cellular telephones, computers, video recorders, fax machines or pagers. Electronic communication has the same meaning as the term defined in Subsection 12 of Section 2510 of Title 18 of the United States Code.

Criminal Threats Defenses—California Penal Code Section 422: Defending Charges of Criminal Threats Under California Penal Code Section 422.

Depending on the facts and circumstances of your case, a skilled criminal defense attorney may be able to argue that the alleged threat does not meet the criteria of a criminal threat set forth in California Penal Code Section 422.

Ambiguous Statement

A threat that was ambiguous or lacks sufficient credibility as being serious is not sufficient to be considered as a criminal threat.

Vague Statement

A threat that was only a vague statement without the prospect of execution of the statement made is not sufficient to be considered a criminal threat.

Not Imminent

A threat is not considered a criminal threat if there is no evidence that [the possibility of] a physical confrontation was actually or reasonably imminent.

No Requisite Fear

A threat cannot be a criminal threat if the person threatened never feared for his or her own safety or for his or her family's safety.

Fear Unreasonable

A threat cannot be a criminal threat if the person's fear was unreasonable.

The words used and the surrounding circumstances will be considered in making this determination. If it was not reasonable, the defendant can use this as a viable defense.

Only Momentary Fear

A threat cannot be a criminal threat if the person's fear was only momentary.

Again, this was before "terrorist" had the connotation it has today. Now they simply call it "criminal threats," but back in the day, they wheeled out the moniker "terrorist threats" to give it a certain panache.

Once I found out she was deaf, I had a new and fresh problem to confront. Communication. Apparently, she refused to use a sign-language interpreter in court. She decided she was going to speak directly to the court, but no one understood what she said, and she could not hear, so it was a total disaster. Flustered and petrified of looking like a bad guy pushing around an old deaf woman defending the honor of her poor murdered dog was more than the judge could handle, so he continued the case and called me.

My only line of communication was the phone relay system. Another interpreter told me that it existed and how to use it. A phone call would come from me to a third-party "relayer," who would listen to what I said, type it out, and send it live to the lady, who would then type back to the interpreter, who would then read her responses, and this was how we were supposed to communicate.

Sounded simple enough. Time consuming, but simple enough. So I sent her a letter introducing myself and explaining that the court had appointed me to help her. I defined my role as her advocate and told her when I was going to call her and that I would do everything I could to help her. At the time and date noted, I got on the relay system and pretended I knew how it worked. Before I knew it, my new client was on the other end. It went something like this:

"Hello, Ms. J, my name is David Slomovic, and I am here to help you."

Long pause as I hear typing in the background.

I then heard a disapproving sound, almost a grunt from the relay person.

"Fuck you!" she relayed to me. "I don't need your fucking help."

I don't know who was more stunned, me or the relayer, but it was pretty close.

Blindsided by the hostile deaf lady, I cleared my throat. This was going to be a little more daunting than I thought.

"Ms. J, let me say from this moment on that you are not ever going to use profanity with me or anyone else in this criminal matter, as you are already facing charges that, in theory, could put you in jail for many years, so I suggest you drop the vulgar language and give me some information so, as your attorney, I can focus on trying to defend you and keep from being convicted and going to jail. Do we understand each other?"

More typing sounds. I felt good about this return volley and knew that we would now get down to it, and I would have regained control of the situation.

Very slowly, the relayer read to me the following: "Fuck you and everything you said. I don't want you and I can already tell you are terrible. Go to hell, cocksucker."

I was stunned. I had dealt with some pretty bad and rough people in my life, but nothing had prepared me for her. I sensed even the relayer thought I should throw in the towel here. This was embarrassing. I getting my ass kicked by an old deaf lady, but I couldn't fight back. And not only that, she had an audience who had no choice but to read me every word, somehow doubling the torture and humiliation of it all.

I wondered how I would feel if I got on her level. But I flashed forward, and standing before the court listening to the transcript of me bawling out the old deaf lady being read was something I did not want to experience. She had me on my heels. I had to outmaneuver her and needed to do it now. I took a deep breath and went for broke.

"What was the name of your dog? How long had you had it?"

Typing sounds.

There was a very long silence. Probably close to half a minute. I sensed I had gotten around her Maginot line.

Slowly, the relay girl said, "Sandy. Girl. Twelve years."

That was it. It was all over. I had reached her.

I told her I had had a dog, that my father forced me to name it PooPoo after my sister's dog who had run away, and how much I loved the dog but hated that name. That I understood the pain of that loss, and that I would do everything to seek justice for Sandy, but I needed her help and I needed her to answer some questions for me.

Typing sounds, followed by a long pause of emptiness.

"He killed my dog. I am not going back to court. I am not going to jail. Go fuck yourself." This was followed by the relay girl stating, "Your conversation is over. The other party has completed the call and is no longer connected with you."

You're telling me. That call was the high point of our relationship.

I went to work. I read over everything, listened to what I could, and tried to figure out a way to keep this sad little old lady from getting convicted on all counts.

She would likely never do jail time, but I still wanted to help her. That was my job, but there was so much evidence stacked against her, and she was not denying any of it. Then the prosecutor on the case made a serious mistake. He threatened me. He said to me something like, "You know if she fights the case and is convicted on all counts, I will have to demand some jail time so she knows she cannot just fuck with people and the system."

He just had to make it personal. Until that point, she was a nasty, old, mean, crazy, deaf dog lady who needed a Xanax. But he was going to pursue jail time and punish her for exercising her rights to defend herself in this deranged reaction of loss? She needed counseling, not to be in a cell with real criminals. Just bringing that up as an option angered me and provided all the motivation I needed to seek a miracle to save the deaf dog lady.

I worked the case up and down, and it was an obvious loser. They had her every which way. Between the phone records, the multiple witnesses, and the distinctive voice, she was cooked. So I did what I always did with a new and relatively unusual charge. I went back to basics and checked out the annotated codes and the jury instructions.

I found an annotation in the supplement that stated that the restraining order had to be in place *prior* to any of the calls in order to qualify for the 422 charge. I checked the restraining order. It was valid, but it was dated *after* all the calls had taken place. She had continued to make the calls after the TRO, but the specific charges that they brought were dated prior to the TRO. Their case had no merit. This was a miracle finding. My plan was to blindside them in trial and win a directed verdict. I brought it to my boss to make sure I had it right, and with an ear-to-ear smile, he told me I was amazing and to enjoy humiliating the city attorney.

I had a decision to make. Do I do the trial, get the statistic that bosses loved (that would help me with promotions), and win in glory, risking that a whacked-out judge could just ignore the law, which happens, while having to sit beside Little Miss Sunshine while she curses everyone out? Or do I go to the prosecutor, have a "come to Jesus" meeting with him, and give him the quick and honorable opportunity to dismiss the case and save face? He would dismiss and refile if she continued, but that would be some other lawyer's problem. There was no way for him to win this one, and he would know it.

I decided to make the best move for the client and sit with the CA. He sat down and said, "What's up?" And I tossed over the supplemental instructions that contained the missing element of his case highlighted in yellow. He read them in silence, trying to figure it out. His face was in total confusion. I tossed him the police report so he could connect the dots. Finally, he realized that he made a major mistake that was fatal to his case. He swallowed hard. I just stared into his eyes, enjoying the delicious moment.

It took him probably a minute and a half after reviewing everything before he said a word. Before speaking, he started shaking his head in disapproval. "I'll just refile or she can plead to one, and I'll give her probation. She has to leave him alone."

I looked at him like you would look at a dog that eats its own poop. "I am going to have the case called up in the morning, and you are going to dismiss all counts. Refile, don't refile, your call, but she walks and I will be done. I can make a big long speech in court about your mistake and embarrass you and make the judge make you do it, or you can just walk in and dismiss. Your call."

Next day he came to the court, asked for a sidebar, and explained it in the best way he could to the judge, and the case was dismissed. Quietly. Effortlessly. The judge later called me over for a sidebar and, with the hugest smile, said, "You're fucking unbelievable. Only you could have done that." I walked away in bliss. I had defeated the CA in such brutal fashion that he tapped out and submitted. I had won the case for this lady against incredible odds, and I had banked an invisible and theoretical get-out-of-jail-free card from the judge to use when the right client deserved it.

I walked back to the office and decided to call my client, as she had refused to return to court, and the judge did not really want her there. I got a different relay person this time, another lady. I explained that I had researched every element of the case and found this flaw and that I had gotten all of the charges dismissed and that she had won the case. I congratulated her on the dismissals, advised her to cease making these calls, gave her my sincere condolences on Sandy, and wished her well. Her response?

"Drop dead, you asshole."

"You are very welcome, ma'am." And with that, I was done with the Dead Dog Deaf Lady case. This was the reality of law in its most real, most raw form. That is the sea I swam in for years, and the bottom line is that she probably got off the phone with me and got right back to calling the vet again. I was not having aha Perry Mason moments in which the witness confesses on the stand, as I had imagined as a kid. I was not saving the world or even living the glamorous *LA Law* lifestyle, and it sure did not feel like I was healing or saving anyone.

Chapter 21
DREAM MAKERS

This book has detailed many of the things that are wrong or confusing about senior living, as well as how seniors too often are negatively viewed and represented poorly, with their needs an afterthought at best. What does it look like when seniors are positively represented and treated beautifully, and their needs and wants are the most important thing of all?

The concept of treating the residents of a community like they truly are family members is what inspired me to galvanize our activities program. Just about 99 percent of all activity departments are the same. They did the same things, celebrated the same events, had the same parties, and even hired the same entertainers. How did I know this? Because I mystery shopped all of my competitors, saw what they were doing, and analyzed their monthly newsletters.

I saw a huge opportunity. Virtually no thought was going into this critical space, and to me, the area seemed ripe for new blood and new ideas.

The activities department was the most important area in which I could have an immediate impact. Food, care, maintenance, and housekeeping are all important, of course, but better people than I knew those spaces to a deeper level than I ever would. The one area in which my crazy ideas could flourish related to entertainment and reconnecting people to people and things they cared about. Other staff was taking care of the residents' bodies and apartments, so I wanted to help their souls. So I came up with a plan. First, I installed flat-screen TVs and had rotating pictures and videos of our events so the first thing people saw when they walked in was not an older building but all of the exciting things going on. Now all I had to do was figure out exciting things to do and then have pictures taken.

This was not as easy as it sounds. Seniors are known for wanting things, getting them, and then not wanting them after all. Speaking with them directly and having unannounced focus groups allowed me to casually get to the truth. The truth was that seniors liked activities in which they could not fail or be embarrassed and where they did not have to stick with a schedule. This realization was a breakthrough that explained many of my previous activity failures. For example, residents loved Wii bowling when I introduced it and showed them how to play. All they had to do was swing their arm. But they hated and rejected Wii Brain Academy because they got scored down for failing to accomplish timed tasks.

Seniors strive to avoid embarrassment more than any age group I know.

I birthed a concept called **Senior Boot Camp**, which I believed was a perfect idea. Great speakers on a variety of topics chosen by residents came in and gave amazing lectures to our residents and outside guests (whom I hoped would become residents). The event was a smash hit that day, but zero residents signed up to follow through on any of the topics related to issues they had listed as important to them, mostly because it involved actual work and commitment.

Parties were the low-hanging fruit of activities. I threw great Hawaiian luaus, St. Patrick's Day parties, Fourth of July BBQs, and, of course, a massive Christmas party, the biggest event of the year. But my two favorite and most successful ways of giving residents what they needed but could not do for themselves were the **Senior Olympics** and **Dream Makers**.

The **Senior Olympics**, which we did every year for over five years, was a series of participatory events that included opening ceremonies, dozens of competitions over two weeks, and, of course, the closing ceremonies, where medals were given out to residents based on performance and participation. Our feeling was that you were a winner just by participating, and we managed year after year to approach 90 percent participation. We could not get 90 percent of the residents to agree on what color the sky was, so this was quite a feat. The musical theme of the Olympics would play in the halls for weeks before the games, and we put the Olympic creed on the public-area screens every day: "**The most important thing in the Olympic games is not to win, but to take part; just as the most important thing in life is not the triumph, but the struggle. The essential thing is not to have conquered, but to have fought well.**"

As I had been a Greco-Roman history major, this stuff was music to my ears. To the residents, it was something to talk about, "train for," and look forward to, and a way to grow younger. It inspired them, and the staff, in a way you would not believe, inspiring effort and making the entire building come alive. I cannot describe the pure joy, pride, and comradery we witnessed year after year. We saw people who had been given up on or left for dead who now won or medaled in competitions. It was truly beautiful.

We ordered special T-shirts each year with our logo, and the residents wore them with pride for months. At the closing ceremonies, family and friends showed up to see their residents get their medals. The best part of all was sincerely congratulating the residents, honoring their performances and efforts, and seeing them cheer for each other, watching them high-five, and give huge hugs. It bonded them deeply. It was one huge family supporting each other's perseverance, and it was simply priceless.

Another activity I introduced was **Horse Therapy**. Behind our community was a pristine horse trail, and once day a lady was riding by on her horse. We spoke, and she agreed to bring a couple of horses to the entrance, and residents could feed them carrots and pet them. Petting animals is extremely therapeutic, and we often had dog and rabbit therapy, but my guess was that no other community had horse petting. This ended up being an amazing activity and produced a magnificent moment, maybe my all-time favorite SL moment. A lady struggling with losing her sight, had become angry at life and the world and everyone in it. She had become lost in herself, and losing her sight was a cruel twist that had broken her spirit. I urged her to attend the event and then left her alone. I watched as the residents met and greeted the horses. She slowly stood up and reached for a horse standing about ten feet away. She seemed to call the horse over with mental telepathy, and the horse walked up and nestled its nose beneath her hand. It looked as if they were communicating in some private language, as the horse drew closer until its face was touching her. She closed her eyes and brought her face cheek to cheek with the large animal. They stood there, together, connected in a magical way. Everyone stopped and watched. She kissed the horse on its snout, and they both closed their eyes. She was crying.

I went over and softly put my hand on her back. With tears in her eyes, she told me she was originally from Oklahoma or Kansas, I cannot recall which one, and grew up on a horse ranch. She told me she had not been next to a horse in close to seventy years and that she could not remember being as happy as she was in that moment. We stood there for a while, and it felt like all the pain and anger just melted away. It was a moment burned into my mind. That is what SL should be about.

That moment inspired an idea that percolated in me for years. What if I could help other seniors fulfill a yearning or return to something they missed, or scratch an itch they had never been able to reach? Give them something they have yearned for but were never able to achieve. What if SL became the time in one's life when we finally help make their dreams actually come true?

This was the origin of my favorite creation, **The Dream Makers**. Staff would interview individual residents to find out what they had always wanted to do but never had, or help them connect with someone or something from their past, or take up that hobby they always dreamed of. We could be the instrument of fulfillment for them, and they would get to close a chapter on something in their life they otherwise never would have closed. It would be a fulfillment project of the highest level.

Dream Makers was not about money. It was purely about helping someone, and that was what I most loved about it. We had zero idea if it would work or what the residents would want.

Initially, the staff did the interviews, but it was a total flop. No one understood my concept or had my interviewing skills so I had to do it myself. The first person I interviewed was a sweet gentleman for whom I had a lot of respect. A humble man, he seemed almost embarrassed by my offer. But he looked down and away and drifted off into thought after I made my presentation. Something had come to mind when I asked if there was something he wanted to do but had not done. He lifted his gaze and looked me in the eyes the way only a World War II vet can. "There is something," he said.

He proceeded to explain that the anniversary of his beloved wife's passing was coming up, and she was buried over a hundred miles away. What he most wanted, and what had been on his mind for weeks, was to go there and place a bouquet of flowers on her grave on the one-year anniversary of her passing. I did not think I could be more impressed by someone, but he proved me wrong. I told him I would look into it and get back to him soon.

While the request was unexpected, it was deep, and it became my mission to make this happen. This is exactly what this concept was designed for; though, if you gave me a hundred guesses, I never would have guessed this particular scenario.

The burial site was too far for our van to go on the day he needed, so we researched limo services and tried to figure out a way to lower costs so we could send him in style and comfort. One company agreed to do it gratis based on the circumstances. I paid for the flowers myself, and they were going to be waiting for him when he arrived at the site, as would a golf cart to take him directly to the gravesite and avoid any trips or falls. When I told him we were set and all he had to do was walk out the front door and take the ride, he stoically shook my hand and walked away.

To me, this was exactly what he deserved and precisely what SL should be all about—assisting seniors in doing things that are important to them.

The next person I interviewed was a woman. She was a wonderful sweet widow from back east, probably close to her nineties. When I interviewed her about her dream, I could see her eyes twinkle and her mind engage. When I asked her what it was, she smiled and said, "It's nothing." I asked her if she felt comfortable sharing it with me. After staring into my eyes, she relaxed her body language and told me her story.

When she was a teenager back in New York, she met a boy. He was a handsome and charming man but came from a divorced home, so her parents forbade her from having a relationship with him. Still, there was something very special about him, and they secretly saw each other until World War II, when he was drafted. She never saw or heard from him again. She always assumed he had been killed in the war, and she always wanted to know what his fate was so that she could finally close the door on that chapter.

She eventually moved on, met a wonderful man, and had a family and a wonderful life. But it always gnawed at her that she never knew where and when and how he passed away.

She gave me his name and approximate birthdate and thanked me for listening and for allowing her to get it off her chest. I felt bad for her, but at least she had the chance to release that pent-up story. The next day I got to my office, googled the name, and *bam*, there he was. There was his exact name, in a similar location, with the approximate age she had given, plus a phone number. My heart skipped a beat. Could this really be him?

I called the activities director and told her what had happened. She was speechless. I asked her to call the number, explain the situation, and see if it could be true. She called me back quickly and said that a woman had answered and stonewalled her. No info. No idea if this was the real McCoy.

So I called. The same woman answered. I explained who I was, about my community, what I was doing, and why I was calling. She was having none of it. But in the background I heard an older male voice say, "Ask him what her nickname was." I told the woman I did not know she had a nickname. She said to call back with the nickname so he would know this was for real. Fair enough.

I called the resident and asked what her nickname had been. She asked why, so I explained. "Oh, my God. That is so like him. It must be him. What kind of a life has he had?" I explained that I did not get past the girl, who sounded like a middle-aged daughter. She told me the nickname, and I promised to call her back. I called

New York and told the daughter the nickname. She repeated it to the man. Suddenly, he took the phone.

"Is this real?"

I explained to him that yes, it was real, who I was and the entire story. I asked his permission to connect them. There was silence. Then he softly said, "I assumed she was dead."

"She is very much not dead, sir, but until fifteen minutes ago, she spent the last sixty years believing you were the one who was dead."

I could hear and feel the deep breath he took. "Have her call me at nine New York time tomorrow morning. I will be ready. Thank you and good-bye."

I felt a warm happiness bubble appear inside my heart. I called her back and told her. She was thrilled, but said she was not sure what she would wear. I reminded her that it did not matter since they would only be on the phone.

"Of course, of course. I can't believe it. I feel wonderful. It is so exciting. This is like being queen for a day." I gave her the number and wished her luck.

The next day, they spoke for the first time since 1944. She described it as an amazing experience, and that she was happy that he had a good life. She sounded so happy. I was proud to have played a small part in this. Thank God for Google.

The story spread through the staff like wildfire. They loved that the sweet woman had closed that chapter of her life. Everyone was lifted by it, and although finding lost loves was not part of my original plan, it seemed like the perfect extension of the concept. I told people the story at dinners and at meetings. Men thought it was brilliant. Women cried with joy. I had hit the mother lode.

I interviewed the next resident, a spunky gentleman whom I enjoyed very much. He wanted two things. One was to be on the cover of a Wheaties box. The second was to find his first girlfriend, whom he nearly married. I was seeing a bit of a theme in what the seniors thought about but never spoke of out loud.

We contacted Wheaties, and they thought it was a joke. I explained we were not joking, and they said they would get back to me. I only wanted him on one box. We located his ex-girlfriend in about ten seconds. We set it up, and they had their magical moment as well.

The next turn went to a lovely and sweet couple originally from Cuba. When I interviewed them, all they wanted was to go back and see his hometown and his church one last time. I had explained to him, as I did to all at the very beginning, that this was not "Make A

Wish" where we would get donations and fly people to places or have a meeting with a celebrity. But all he wanted was to go and see his beloved neighborhood and church one more time. So I did the only thing I could think of. I got his old address, entered it into Google Earth and *boom*, we were flying over Cuba. As Google Earth descended over Cuba, their eyes lit up, and when it pulled up a photo of where his old home used to be, he almost did not seem to care that the old house was gone. We pivoted around the neighborhood, and he started to recognize sites. But the enchanting moment was when I found his old church, and we saw it together. The tears filled both their eyes. We were no longer there with them; they were alone in their own world. She in her wheelchair, he in a chair, with them both tenderly holding hands smiling, pointing, and laughing. The activity director was wiping tears. This, my friends, is what SL should be.

These vignettes are just a sampling of what happens when we stop treating seniors like fragile vases and engage them in life. These magical moments changed me and marked the fulfillment of the complete transformation from my criminal law life. I had found my nirvana in their joy.

But all that glitters is not gold. In almost each case, my high was shattered.

Regarding the man who wanted to go to the cemetery, what I did not tell you was that, a few days before the event, a staff member called me and explained there was a problem. He had shared with his family what we were doing for him. To our amazement, they were deeply offended.

They said that they should have been the ones to do it for him, not us, that this was an internal family matter, and that we had no place in it. I was stunned. They wanted to know why we were doing this. The new Dream Makers program was explained to them. They asked why he did not ask them, his family, to do this. My staff wanted to know my response. I told them that we did this because we are in the happiness business and experimenting with this new idea, and when I asked him what we could do to make him happier, this is what he asked us for. We had no intention to trouble or upset anyone. The exact opposite. When pressed as to why he told *us* and did not tell *them*, I asked them when the last time was that they had asked him what they could do to make him happier. We were instructed to cancel the limo and the flowers, and they would take him themselves. They took him, and we never discussed it again.

Regarding the lady who found her old flame in New York, the story got such traction in my world that I decided to create a marketing campaign around it. "Come to Sunnycrest, where dreams really do come true…"

I met with the lady and explained how many people had loved the story and were inspired, and I knew people were reaching out to family and friends and mending fences and reconnecting all because of her. She did not smile. I asked why. She told me that she did not want the story further publicized, that she and the man had decided that they did not intend to stay in contact, which surprised me since I had gathered he was a widower. I was confused. She had been so excited and happy. What had changed? She avoided the question when I asked her why. I did not pry.

Stunned, I walked away. This did not make sense at all. Then the activities director or some other staff, who had been watching me speak to her in the lobby and saw my face, came over and explained it to me. Apparently, she had decided that her children and family should never know that she loved someone before their father. She thought it might hurt them or make them think she only married her husband because she thought the love of her life was dead.

The man who had asked me to find his old girlfriend also, I was told, had his reunion disconnected by his family. They did not like what we had done either. He ended the involvement, and I was told it was his daughters who ended it although I do not know that for a fact. The concern was fraud or undue influences. I think, at the core, all these people are loved by their family, but their families want them to be independent...until they are.

Dream Makers was designed to bring joy to my seniors. It worked beautifully. In fact, it worked much better than I had imagined, but it never occurred to me that family would be so territorial and turn a beautiful innocent positive into a negative. If I had to do it all again, I know how I would fix this flaw, but for someone with such good intent, I would be lying if there was no admission that all this frustrated me and left a very bad taste in my mouth. Everyone talks about how seniors should be adored and cared for, but when I did something about it, I became Al Capone. For the love of God, when do seniors get to put themselves first? When?

Chapter 22
THE CRITICAL CONVERSATION NO ONE HAS

If you have read this book in linear order, by now you have more information and knowledge about senior living than 90 percent of the executive directors running communities, and possibly more than many of the people who run these companies. You may not have the numbers, graphs, degrees, or years, but you know the soul of senior living in a truer way than most people running senior living. You have touched the core of the system, looked behind the curtains, and even under the hood and faced difficult facts. The journey has not been an easy or predictable one, but by now you are locked and loaded with information and knowledge, and you will not be anyone's sucker now or in the future. You are now able to make intelligent decisions for you and your loved ones, and that makes me deeply happy. This should be a transparent and open path for the family and the senior, and not the hall of mirrors it has been made into. Seniors deserve the respect and clarity I am seeking to provide. That is the way it should be.

But now that you are *here*, I must tell you are you not *there* yet. There is one huge hurdle that must be overcome, and it is the one conversation almost no one has, and for those who have it, it is rarely done right. So here is the playbook to get it right the first time.

Go with the truth. It is critical that you speak honestly and realistically to the person who is going to be moving into this new world. The number two reason that these transitions fail almost always from day one is that the resident has been so hyped up by family and the community that they expect Shangri-La. They expect Shangri-La and get Boise. No disrespect to Boise, I hear it is great, but it is not Shangri-La.

Family after family builds the new home into something it is not. It is not "home," at least not initially. Most people who do not understand this space imagine senior living to be a hospitality play. It is not a "hotel" that Mom or Dad is moving into. It is not Disneyland for seniors or a cruise ship that never leaves dock. It is simply an apartment building designed around seniors, with extra benefits and hopefully a capable safety net, and it should be explained honestly and factually. Let us be clear. Most residents do not want to move in. At my peak of success, we had over 140 residents living happily in my building, and not one had wanted to move in. Not one.

They ended up being very happy. Better than happy. Belonging.

But it did not start out that way. They came in afraid, scared, and sad.

They have heard their whole life, and seen in many cases, that this was "the final stop." Seniors are not stupid. They know what you are doing, and they deserve the respect to get it straight. Believe me, they can take it.

The mistake most families make is they oversell what Mom or Dad is going to get, specifically how much staff attention there will be. Most places introduce you to everyone they can find on staff to amaze you with how many people will be there for you. So people move in and call the front desk and want a lightbulb changed or fresh towels or room service or see a bug, and when the cavalry does not come quickly, the smile fades, the "you lied" or "I told you so" phone call to the family hits, and then calls or e-mails to the staff begin. The goodwill vibe never returns. Nervous parents enflame tense children, and the opportunity for a smooth transition gets soured quickly and perhaps permanently. I cannot tell you how many families have had this happen. It is all because they never had "the talk" about realistic expectations in senior living.

Here is what should be explained:

First: Mom or Dad (or both) should be told to think of this as a private apartment like in an apartment building. What is special here is that all the meals are served and included, and everything that is broken gets fixed for free.

Second: Explain that there is housekeeping, but usually done seriously once a week. The "maid service" is not daily, like in a hotel. Many communities, but not all, have free or coin laundry machines as well. I kept mine free to encourage residents to do it themselves. That is a good, solid way to maintain an air of independence.

Third: Everyone on staff will not jump the moment you call, even if you say it is urgent. That is because everyone calls and says everything is urgent. If

TIP: I cannot justify this conclusion, but in my personal experience, people who do their own laundry tend to stay mentally fit longer. There is something positive about doing laundry that I cannot explain, but doing it is calming and a reflection of self-esteem and privacy boundaries, and somehow the people who did it always seemed to keep their edge. Just an opinion. This is coming from someone who has not done his own laundry since Reagan was in office, so take this with a healthy grain of salt.

255

you sit in the lobby and hear the receptionist get "urgent" call after call, you will know what I mean. People pull the emergency pull cords when they cannot find their remote or if they want to learn what is for lunch. React accordingly.

Fourth: The food will be good. Not amazing. Not Michelin five star, but good, nutritious, and most likely plentiful. Food is the number-one conversation topic in most communities, and everyone likes different things, so expect occasional complaints and dissatisfaction. A call from Mom that the beef stroganoff was lousy should not result in triggering DEFCON 2.

Fifth: The care will not be perfect. He or she will love some of the caregivers and some not so much. The favorite caregivers are beloved by all, and requested by all as well. Realize that you may not always get "Joy," the perfect caregiver, every time, and try not to be upset if they bring a new lady to train or to give you assistance. Even Joy was new once. Look at it as an opportunity to train the person being trained. Remember, you are the client.

Sixth: Realize that as much as the staff might adore and respect you, it does not mean they have all night to listen to your stories or inner thoughts. I recognize that this might sound a little harsh, but seniors *love* to talk, and if a caregiver has five people to bathe during a shift and you just absolutely love talking about what is going on with your grandson in the army, know that the reason he or she cut you off is not disrespect or indifference; it is the demands of the job. Everyone says, "Well, you should hire more people and have more staffing so they have more time." Sure, but whenever there is even the slightest fee increase, you should hear the howling. Just know that part of keeping your rates down is having efficiencies, and that includes staff needing to respond to others in need, too. Staff should not ever rush you, but, at the same time, they cannot sit for tea and lollygag either.

Seventh: They are not going to love every other resident or hit it off immediately with most. Many communities have at least one hundred residents, so there are going to be people you like and people you do not like. An SL community is very much like regular life, just in smaller portions. Create the expectation that there will be preexisting cliques and groups, and people who have been there longer will know each other. Everyone came in knowing no one. They are not excluding her; they just do not know her. It is never fun being the new kid, even at eighty, so, if possible, scout the place for someone your parent knows, someone from church, work, or neighborhood. Ask around, speak to your pastor or anyone with information and try to find a link. A familiar face will go a long way.

Examine the newsletter for activities. See which he or she shows interest in and then come to a few *before* move-in. Get them to know one or two friendly people and know her apartment number so you can figure out who her neighbors are. Most importantly, get to know the activities director. Getting in good with this person will be very helpful to your family member. Volunteer to assist the activities director in an event, or donate some ribbons or balloons or gift baskets so she can save part of her budget for other things. Donate those art supplies cramming up your garage, and you might find that you not only clear space and help her out but that your mom or dad becomes a favorite of the AD.

Meet the new neighbors in advance. Maybe even bring a little gift, like a home-baked muffin or fake plant or something. It might not be a love connection, but it is a good first impression.

Eighth: Explain that if they are not happy with where they are sitting in the dining room, it is not permanent. In some places, you sit wherever you'd like, and that can be good or bad. This goes back to the importance of finding a friendly face to sit with. The dining room is the equivalent of the school yard, where lines are drawn and groups hang out. Being on the outs is not where you want them. All you need is one or two people to assist them in getting acclimated.

Ninth: Make nice with the hairdresser. She is a secret key to success. Ladies, in particular, must get along with the lady who does their hair. To guys, this sounds crazy, but this is critical. Introduce the resident to the hairdresser when she is not busy and pay her a little extra on the side to take extra care of your special person to get things off on the right foot. Same goes with the driver. Important relationships that no one ever considers.

Tenth: Do not make the mistake of saying this is "temporary" or a "trial." Once you tell some people it is temporary, they never buy in and make an effort. They may also think that if they continue to complain, you will crack and finally agree for them to live with you, or give in and agree they should go back home and have more care. It is very important that they try to make this work, because, if they get past the first month, they will be great. Remember how I told you no one in my happy building ever wanted to come in the first place? Well, some came in kicking and screaming only to later love it and feel more at home than you would believe.

Let me tell you about a resident we will call Carol (not her real name). Carol was a tall, thin, spicy lady with orange skin, wild red hair, and a mouth with no filter. Her daughter, a nurse, moved Carol into my community after Carol had nearly died in her home alone. Carol was feisty beyond belief, and during my daily walkaround, she caught me and said, "Hey, you the owner?"

When I replied yes, she said, "I want to tell you something. I don't want to be here. My darn daughter is forcing me to be here, and I want to be alone at my house and not here with all these strange people, and I want out, and nothing you can say is gonna change my mind. What do you think about that?"

I had heard she was a pistol and having trouble acclimating. "Then I think you should leave," I said.

"What?" She seemed shocked by my response.

"I said I think you should leave. I don't want people here who do not want to be here. You are free to leave whenever you choose. But I do not want someone here who will pollute those who have chosen to be here and are happy. We don't need you or anyone with such a bad attitude. People are here to be happy, not to be attacked the way you just attacked me."

She was stunned. She must have expected me to beg her to stay or offer her the moon and the stars. The last thing she expected was to be told to leave. By the end of the conversation, she was arguing with me why she should not leave. I let her win that argument.

Carol did not understand that she had a role to play that would bring her joy. I could not explain it to her; she had to experience it. She was a very sweet person who simply did not know how to integrate, as she was put there with no strategy and not by her own choosing. She needed, like I believe all seniors do, a purpose.

The next time I saw her, I said, "Still here?" Carol was very smart. She had figured it out on her own. "I help take care of the other residents, and I help the staff at breakfast, too." Carol was a tremendously warm and giving lady who deeply enjoyed serving others and helping people adjust to the new world. She was so good and special, in fact, that Carol ended up becoming one of my elite ambassadors and one of my favorite clients ever. She also ended up meeting someone she felt very close to and had a meaningful and unexpected relationship that provided her true companionship. She simply had not known she could be happy once again.

Expectations are everything in life but even more so during this transition—you only get one shot at a first impression. Failure—people who move in but soon move out—did occur, usually because of a failure of expectations.

Another reason is lack of planning. Sometimes the community simply drops the ball. Someone moves in, and all elements of the apartment are not ready, or a place in the dining room has not been set (seating is often assigned), or the TV does not work, or the shower head is not installed, or a special diet has not been communicated to the chef, or meds did not arrive on time, or on day one the care staff misses the new resident on the list of those who need to be ambulated to the dining room. Little things that feel like big things.

While all of these things can be quickly corrected, they leave a bad taste in everyone's mouth. So I am going to give you three simple suggestions free of charge to make move-in go smoothly and start the new life off on the right foot.

1. Do a dry run. Walk through the facility with a staff member, get the keys and make sure they work, see where parking is, check that the meds are in, make sure the new resident is on the assistance list if applicable, check for an assigned seat in the dining room, and make sure that the name on the apartment door is

spelled correctly. All little things, but big things to your family member.

2. Blow up a favorite picture and tack it to the door of the new apartment. A nice big, "We Love You" sign with photos of the grandkids goes a long way, too.

3. *Never* move in on the weekend. I know it is more convenient, but the A-team tends to work Monday to Friday. People love to move in on the weekend, but take a day off work, and do it when the staff you have been talking to and working with are present. This practice cuts down on the failure rate and helps new residents settle in faster.

Listen closely. Moving into senior living is not like having Ed McMahon knock on the door to tell you that you have won the Publisher's Clearing House sweepstakes. It is a tough transition that can be made smoother *if* expectations are realistic and communicated properly. The steps I shared with you are based on mistakes I and others have made, so you can benefit from our experiences.

The last piece of advice I am going to give you is to visit frequently, especially in the beginning. The psychology is that residents fear that they are being dumped or abandoned. As silly as that may sound, it is true more often than one would think. Temper that with making plans to visit before they even move in. Human nature is to fear change, and by making plans and visiting often, much anxiety will be diffused.

At the beginning of this chapter, I stated that the number two reason these transitions fail from day one is that the resident has been so hyped up by family and the community that when they actually move in, they expect Shangri-La. You may have been wondering what the number-one reason is. That, my friends, is found in the next chapter.

Chapter 23
THE MISTAKE WE NEVER REALIZE OR ADMIT

In this brief chapter, I will focus on the touchiest of subjects in an attempt to explain why seniors often refuse to move, move and refuse to stay, or move out without giving any real effort. You may not like the answer.

I certainly do not.

The number-one reason these transitions fail almost from day one is something that we never realize or admit. Some think it is "helicopter children" hovering over their parent, and that the family is to blame because they cannot balance their emotional needs—they either push the community too strongly or do not push the resident strongly enough for it to work and unconsciously sabotage it.

Another theory is that the community is to blame. While a community is never perfect, there will undoubtedly be happy people there, and the community gets credit for that just as it gets blamed for unhappy ones.

My belief is that it is simply about the residents themselves. Sometimes their peers are gone, their love has passed, they have lost hope, or in all honesty, they just do not want to continue living and have surrendered to the sands of time. The last thing they want is a new transition. No more challenges. They feel they simply do not have the strength. Sometimes they have lost their faith. Sometimes their faith drives them to want to reach the end so they will see loved ones or no longer feel pain.

Some people just run out of life. Living is no longer a gift. One person told me it was a curse. He had outlived his spouse. He had outlived his siblings. He had even outlived his children. "Why I am still here, I have no idea," he told me. It broke my heart.

Purpose. Everyone needs a purpose, especially men. Deprived of one, people lack direction and a sense of belonging to something bigger. Every day is like the one before it, and days and weeks and months fly by without contribution or reward. One loses one's sense of identity, and this is where society has blown it. On one hand, we have a reservoir of seniors with a wealth of experience and wisdom, who sit alone with no one to talk to, and on the other hand, we have a world full of students and new workers who have neither practical experience nor real knowledge. Yet we do not connect them. Why?

The happiest I have ever seen seniors is when they are engaged in some kind of activity with children and young people. This bridge would give that needed connection between generations; it would provide for the critical downloading of wisdom from one generation to another, and assist younger people to appreciate the sacrifices of those who came before them. But we do not do this. Most elderly people are fearful of change and do not want to meet new people if it involves effort. Instead of mentoring others and sharing their life experiences, many choose to live in their little castle and control the drawbridge. One can do everything right, find the right place, and set it all up, but the senior has to want to have a better life, and sometimes does not think it is worth the effort.

We usually never realize that these people have checked out. They do not announce it, but I have seen it. Sometimes an equation is made, or a decision is made, and no promise of a better future is welcome or desired.

I had a great aunt who was active and loved playing cards. She came to us for dinner one time and described to me that she was losing her sight, but card playing was her favorite thing. I wondered what she would do without her card playing. Well, what she did was give up. She stopped eating, went into a coma, and was gone before we knew what had happened. It was shocking. I have seen this happen with spouses when one passes, and the other has a massive medical drop soon after, resulting in them being together again upstairs.

Some older people reach a point at which all the difficulties, challenges, pain, and limitations finally deprive them of the joys in life, and they no longer want a better path. Some are content with what has happened and feel they do not have the strength or stamina for another transition. There is little one can do about this. Certainly, the community cannot create the fire in a person who does not want the warmth. We do not know or want to believe that this is true, but is it possible that the endless tide of glorifying youth, the devotion to looking and feeling young, and the endless barrage of negativity toward aging and seniors has zapped them of the desire to fight? Have they had enough of fighting? Or, like a rock on the beach beaten by the endless surf, have they reached their limit and become too diminished to fight back?

Or perhaps it is a choice. Perhaps people choose a path or choose an attitude. Several years ago, I was in Tel Aviv, Israel, in a beachfront hotel, tossing and turning in bed due to jet lag. I was alone, so I left the hotel and walked up and down the beach thinking about my work and my life. Lost in thought, I sat down on a bench to watch the sunrise, and the sky came alive in a flurry of beautiful and vibrant colors. I was thinking about my business and how to improve it and market it better, and mentally worked on the remodel design that would turn my building into a place of happiness and beauty. I became hypnotized by the magentas, oranges, and yellows of the dawn sky, entranced by their beauty.

I noticed, on the bench beside me, an old Israeli couple also admiring the beautiful sky. They looked ninety and so happy. I asked them what their secret was. They told me that they lived each day like it was their last because they knew that one day they would be right.

I asked how they dealt with growing older. The man told me that they each had lived a full life of working, helping others, having children, and serving the country, and had even lived to see great-grandchildren. "What more could someone want?" they asked. He added that old age was hard because you lose your purpose, agenda, schedule, and goals. He shared that after they do their daily walk on the beach and morning exercise, he makes his wife breakfast (to make up for the lifetime of her making him breakfast every day), and is done with his day by 7:00 a.m. With a glint in his eyes, he added that he used to run a large and successful company, and they always needed him and bugged him and kept him very busy. "But now," he added, "the world somehow survives each day without me making one decision," and he missed it.

I asked the lady, who was smiling as he spoke, what she thought. She said her only hope was that, when they died, they died together, but that life was like a peach born out of a seed. It grows, becomes ripe, then dies by being eaten or by falling, and the seed becomes another peach…and that is life. Then they both got up, said good-bye, and walked away like they had to be somewhere.

I have no idea what the truth is. Ask me when I am ninety, if I make it that far. I will have all the answers, unless, by then, ninety is the new seventy…

Chapter 24
THE END OF THE BEGINNING

In Dante's *Inferno*, he writes that the hottest places in hell are reserved for those who, in times of moral crisis, preserve their neutrality. While that is seen as perhaps a reach in relation to this subject, I submit that too many seniors today are suffering in silent crisis, and that this statement is more true than it is false. Crisis can look like poverty, dementia, physical pain, or even simply the deep silence of depression or isolation.

Today, seniors live with much more fear and loneliness than ever before. This is due in part to people living longer than ever—outliving spouses, peers, and even their children. Seniors are living beyond their own expectations, often kept around by medical intervention and new medicines.

The 1950s and 1960s concept of seniors moving in with their children—which, in many cultures, is a common occurrence—is declining and is not always successful even when it occurs. Seniors want the freedom and independence to do whatever they want whenever they want, but simultaneously want or need a safety net. Layers of complex needs and emotions on top of familial and financial dynamics scare most people away from the best, but not the most obvious, solution.

The real problem is how seniors are viewed by society, which is the opposite of how seniors view themselves. We live in a world that blesses youth above wisdom. The glorification of all that is new and young and shiny comes at the expense of all that is proven. Society has, intentionally or not, condemned and degraded all that is old. We negatively view things that are aged, ancient, and geriatric, and view anyone in that category as feeble, impaired, infirmed, tired, and over the hill. We shower with love all that is new, young, and youthful. We no longer call people "green" or "unseasoned" or "inexperienced." They are "fresh" and "current" and "blossoming."

This wave of ageism is represented by, if not generated by, the barrage of messages we absorb day in and day out on TV, in movies, and in advertisements. The bad news is that we are showered with it daily and no longer realize its impact on us.

This last Thanksgiving, my family and I gathered for the feast, and three generations watched football. A new interesting commercial for PayPal came on that showed several baby boomers sitting at a restaurant when the bill comes. They all throw their credit cards down to split the bill. They are all frowning. The caption reads "Old

Money Is Still Trying to Split the Bill." The next shot cuts to twenty-year-olds racing around in bumper cars smiling from ear to ear. The caption reads "New Money Is Already On to Better Things, Pay Friends Back Faster with New Money." The message is clear. I watched the eyes of my young sons and of Grandpa John. Zero reaction. They all accepted that even something like money can be criticized for being old, and that advertisers had found a way to make spending money fresh, hip, and cool.

When the game came back on, one commentator complimented Anquan Boldin, a wide receiver who played for Florida State and several NFL teams. When he played a great game for the Detroit Lions that Thanksgiving, I was happy for him. So I had to chuckle, right after seeing the PayPal commercial, when their praise focused on how he was still performing despite being so old. "The old guy is still getting it done." Boldin is all of thirty-six.

Granted, in the world of football, thirty-six is not young, but "the old guy"?

This stuff is not a part of the past. It is firmly part of the present.

But the news is not all bad.

That same weekend I saw a commercial aimed at seniors. Two grandparents accidentally see what I think was a Twitter post by their granddaughter stating she was dreading visiting her grandparents' Wi-Fi-less home.

"My grandma's house is straight medieval. She's got no Wi-Fi."

Another pair of elders read a post, "Entering the gates of hell where there is no Wi-Fi and no shows."

In both cases, with surprise and shame on their faces, the grandparents contact Xfinity and get the hook-up. When the granddaughter comes, she is stunned to see that technology did not die at their door, making the grandparent a hero. They share a truly heartwarming holiday together. I loved this commercial because, for once, it looked at seniors as capable of thought and adaptation.

This is only the beginning. At some point soon, we will start to see older people in movies and in shows. As the people who advertise realize this should be their target demographic, things will turn. I predict that sooner rather than later there will be more shows with seniors, more products for them, and even more movies starring seniors. I would say they center, at least initially, on seniors bored with retirement or doing wild things because they no longer have formal responsibilities and just don't care anymore. Older actors who complain they are being shut out will be embraced.

The people who pushed the seniors down and away likely will try to be their advocates now that they are on "the wrong side" of the demographics. See Madonna, the poster girl for trashy underage hypersexuality, now complaining no one wants what she is selling anymore. Perhaps a sixty-year-old worth $560 million singing "Like a Virgin" no longer gets the attention or money she wants, so she is now jumping on the bandwagon and yelling about ageism.

The shift has begun. Almost no one realizes it, but now you are clued in. Clued in to what society has been doing, what the senior-living communities have been doing, and what the seniors themselves have been doing. Now you are armed with so much information and knowledge that you can successfully assist someone you care about in making the best decision possible. **A better life awaits most people in senior living.** And you will enjoy that satisfaction when you are the hero for your family by navigating the choices and hurdles and finding a community in which your loved one can thrive. I have been your Sherpa, taking and guiding you on the journey to the mountaintop so you can do something truly special for someone you love. Because, in the end, that is what we all want for our loved ones. Most of us have been trapped between fear and avoidance when it comes to dealing with parents or grandparents and the realities of aging. **Dealing with aging does not mean pretending it is not happening. It is the opposite.** It is about embracing the incredible nature of the journey while honestly looking at what has changed, and adapting life and/or technology to fit the new reality.

I see aging as a huge opportunity and a huge positive instead of the dramatic negative you have been force-fed your entire life. I envision a world of happy people satisfied with their lives and their journey yet still having something left in the tank. I envision a world in which we honor the past but live with a purpose and an eye toward the future.

That is the mission of this book. That we take the trip together, that we make seniors' dreams come true, that we dream of things that never existed, and why not? If we are lucky enough to go from being the adult child to being the senior, let's hope it is glorious and wonderful and freeing by the time we get there. That it is a beautiful time of life where we make our remaining dreams come true. Where we have a reason to get up and go each day. That we are contributing and still crossing things off our bucket lists and enthusiastic about what will come tomorrow. That we wake up with a smile.

And that is my dream. For all of the wonderful older people I have met in my life who have taught me so much, and been such beacons of light, and who have given so much to so many, do we not owe it to them to make their lives great? Is it so crazy to want to make their golden years truly golden?

My grandmother and my beloved parents filled my life and heart with wisdom, love, and joy. I served them and cherished them the best I could. There is no pain or regret in me, other than what I have shared, for what I could have or should have done. I did all I could when they were here. They now live through me in my actions and in my teaching and training of my children. Our timeless traditions continue.

As we say good-bye for now, remember that every day ten thousand people in the United States turn sixty-five. Every single day. This is the biggest and most expanding market that no one realizes is there. Did everyone else miss the starting gun?

I will end with a request. Trailblaze with me. Join the quest to take care of these people the right way, and to take care of the people who take care of them. We should live lives where the love and pride keeps flowing until the last days without deadlines or boundaries or expiration dates. We should live fully and deeply and passionately at all ages until we hit the wall, but leave nothing in the tank. Take it to the limit and, in the end, give more than we have taken.

If this mission is something that resonates with you, then join me. Instead of waiting for it to magically get better, let us make it better by our own hands. This quest is a giant one, as so much money is being made by those benefiting from sticking seniors into a box and scaring you. Do not be scared. Do not buy the snake oil. Follow your heart, and if you want to take a step in that direction, look at my website (www.unicornseniorliving.com), and follow my Instagram, old_lives_matter. Look for the tiny unicorn, and you will know that it is me.

Finally, the reason I called this book *The Unicorn Project* is because there is a disparity between *what is* and *what should be*. *What is* has been described, analyzed, dissected, and presented to you on a platter. The good and the bad. But the purpose of this book, besides giving you the ultimate insider's view of senior living and the best cheat sheet of all time, is to present what could and should be. Unicorns clearly do not exist. The unicorn is a fabled mythical animal typically represented as a horse with a single straight horn projecting from its forehead. The purpose of naming this new company Unicorn is to show that we can actually create what should be a reality. We can actually create a unicorn by making the lives of seniors better than they can ever dared to even imagine.

51392386R00157

Made in the USA
San Bernardino, CA
21 July 2017